*Trust Your Intuition*

Other books by the same author

**Releasing Your Child's Potential**
*Empower your child to set and reach their own goals*

**Living the Life You Want**
*Your personal key to true abundance
and the richness of everyday life*

Please send for a free copy of the catalogue for full details
(see back cover for address).

# Trust Your Intuition

*Harness the wisdom and power of your inner voice*

2nd edition

Sylvia Clare

**howto**books

First published in 1999 by
How To Books Ltd, 3 Newtec Place,
Magdalen Road, Oxford OX4 1RE, United Kingdom
Tel: 01865 798306 Fax: 01865 248780

Second edition 2002

British Library Cataloguing in Publication Data
A catalogue record for this book is available from
the British Library

Cover design by Baseline Arts Ltd, Oxford

Produced for How To Books by Deer Park Productions
Typeset by PDQ Typesetting, Newcastle-under-Lyme, Staffs.
Printed and bound in Great Britain

Note: The material contained in this book is set out in good
faith for general guidance and no liability can be accepted for
loss or expenses incurred as a result of relying in particular
circumstances on statements made in the book. The laws and
regulations are complex and liable to change, and readers
should check the current position with the relevant
authorities before making personal arrangements.

*I rhyme to set the darkness echoing. . . I rhyme to see myself*

SEAMUS HEANEY:

# Contents

# List of Illustrations

# Preface

Since writing the first edition of this book, I have continued to live by my own advice and have grown and learned so much more. I have found the courage to share my own experiences openly and (a desire fulfilled) to teach and support others as they take their own journeys. I hope these experiences are reflected in this new edition. This book still reflects my own journey to recognise and rediscover my own intuition to ever deeper levels and to rediscover the true wisdom I was born with. Although this is my story, I have since met and worked with many people with the same story to tell and together we have worked to bring them back to their intuitive selves. So this book is also for them.

As a child I knew many things. I knew that you could hear what people were really saying underneath their words, and that people were often dishonest with themselves. I knew that there was a way of life that was based on having fun and working hard but with joy. That you could dig a hole and work really hard but never needed to achieve anything from it, just the experience itself.

I knew that within the walls of my home there was a parallel house, which opened out once you moved into its dimensions to be even bigger than the house I lived in. I knew that my parents weren't my real parents in that they were only for this life. I knew that I had been a child in Africa. And I knew that I had something to say to the world and felt extreme frustration and desperation as all these things were laughed at by those around me, both by my family and my peers at school.

I did not understand that they did not have the same understanding or experiences as I had. I did not understand that everyone could not leave their body at night and go to watch TV or have adventures at will. I did not understand that my parents were afraid of the things I told them, and punished me for making them afraid. I did not understand that others did not see the little energies slipping in and out of plants, and that we really did have 'fairies' in the garden. That sometimes if you spoke to them they would reply. I did not know that other people did not meet the same people in their dreams night after night and that these people would also come in the daytime and talk to them about wisdom and strength and what is real.

Most of all I felt that I was wrong, different, and somehow a bad child. I felt that my parents could not love me as I was, did not like me and would never try to understand me. And perhaps no one ever would.

So from a growing fear of isolation, ridicule and punishment, I gradually lost that knowledge and immersed myself in the reality that everyone else seemed to think was real life. A quiet voice inside me kept telling me that something was terribly wrong with all this, so I learned to be dishonest with myself too.

It took me a long time to wake up again, well into my adult years, when life had confronted me 'yet again' with the fact that I was getting too successful in going down the wrong track 'yet again'.

I have drawn on many sources to explore the subject, from a wide range of views and beliefs that I followed in my search for answers. These experiences changed my life in many ways and I would never return to the isolation of living without intuition because it is so limited. Now I have a way of life that is richer and more rewarding. But the greatest gift it has given me is that I am so much calmer and comfortable in myself that I am able to achieve far more for both myself and for others. Developing an intuitive approach to life has taught me to be gentle, caring and compassionate to both myself and to all those I come into contact with.

Many children are born with very advanced intuitive skills and are taught, as I was, not to trust them. They are taught to believe that only logical, factually-based thought has any validity by the whole education system. Parents and society as a whole tend to dismiss many intuitive experiences as just imagination. Yet if we as a society open to the potential for everyone for find peace and balance in their lives, based on trust and openness. It is there for all and the implications are endlessly positive. Reading this book with an open mind and an inquiring spirit is the first step.

My thanks go to Garner for his guidance, to my sons Matthew and Ben who are both very intuitive and taught me a thing or two, and to Louise who helped me find my own way. Also to all the people who let me use their real stories that illustrate real experiences of intuition. To my publishers, Nikki and Giles, who asked me to write this book. And most of all to my husband David Hughes, who took the trouble to find out who I really am.

*Sylvia Clare*

CHAPTER 1

# Recognising Your Intuition

W ouldn't it be wonderful to find a guidance system that really and honestly helps us find our way through the infinite variety of confusing life experiences? Just imagine being confident:

◆ that you have made the right choices in life
◆ that you can cope with anything that comes your way
◆ that you can see the purpose in everything
◆ that you feel totally connected to your own life.

The irony is that we all have this system in place, but we have not yet learned how to use it fully. We just need to recognise it, to tune in to our intuition. It is that simple, and that hard. Because until we recognise how intuition works, what it is and how to connect with it, it is like putting a six-month-old baby in front of a steering wheel and expecting it to drive down the motorway without having an accident.

The truth is that most people have been tuned out of their intuition and are no longer aware of it – they doubt it, mistrust it, ignore it or even ridicule it. But

> The intuitive mind is a sacred gift and the rational mind is a faithful servant. We have created a society that honours the servant and has forgotten the gift.
>
> (Albert Einstein, 1929)

and I agree with him.

This chapter will tell you how wonderful intuition is, what it is and how to begin reconnecting with yourself in ways that can only make you wonder at their potential – or rather at your potential – the hidden potential that your intuition will show lies within you.

Or you can choose to put this book down and find
something less challenging to read, something that will agree
with your present view of life and confirm that leopards never
can change their spots, the die is cast and old dogs can't be
taught new tricks. So what do you want from your life? What is
the point of living if we don't embrace it fully and find out
how wonderful this thing called living a human life really is –
potentially?

## Learning to know

The word intuition means exactly what it sounds like – in –
tuition – an inner tutor or teaching and learning mechanism
that takes us forward daily. If we let it that is! But, if asked,
would you have to stop and think about:
◆ when you last used your intuition
◆ when you last consciously worked to develop it
◆ when you became aware of how to use it
◆ how to identify an intuitive experience.

And this is where we begin to realise how detached we have
become and why. Where in our life are we taught to act on our
intuitive hunches and gut reactions? Where are we trained to
follow intuitive experiences?

And yet, even without consciously knowing it, we are acting
on our intuition in these simple ways. So how much more
effective could your intuition become if you really followed it?
How far can this thing go?

Well, there is no limit other than the limits you believe in,
the limits your conscious logical mind puts on what is possible,
based on the evidence of experience around you. If Einstein
had thought this way he would never have achieved his
potential either. We all have a potential that is far greater than
we will allow ourselves to believe because we have fallen victim
to the idea that only certain people can achieve like this. Yet,
in our own ways, we can all be achievers. Perhaps we will not
all become Nobel prize winners, but in our own ways we all
have a potential that is far greater than we can imagine and
intuitively we also all know that.

## *Acknowledging cause and effect*

It is important to recognise that you may have dismissed intuitive experiences as pure chance when they occurred. You are certainly far more intuitive than you ever realised and one of the first principles of intuition is to recognise that there is no such thing as chance. Everything occurs as a result of cause and effect. Everything you do, think, believe and feel now will affect your own future. So how do you know what to do now that will create the future you want – how can you make the intuitive choices in life that bring you closer to finding your own potential and living a life that delights and challenges you.

The fact that you are reading this book suggests that you want to know more and sense it within yourself. It is not a coincidence.

You can usefully explore childhood experiences too, and rediscover what you knew then. Many of the points introduced in this first chapter will be explored in depth later on.

## Defining intuition

Intuition is created from lots of received ideas and assumptions, not all of which will be common to everyone. Sometimes intuition is confused with other beliefs, but intuition is not:

- ◆ knowing what and how everything will occur in the future
- ◆ the ability to control situations and people to fulfil your own intentions
- ◆ being able to avoid all difficulties
- ◆ the ability to read other people's minds
- ◆ the ability to be in control of everything around you.

## Experiencing intuition

Intuition is a sense of knowing how to act spontaneously, without needing to know why. The why question leads to indecision, anxiety, caution, and self-limitation. These are all responses which originate in fear of judgement from others, of being wrong or being different.

> Being spontaneous is being able to respond with
> confidence, calmly trusting that whatever the outcome
> you will have a positive if challenging experience that will
> lead to greater self-awareness and joy in life.

Intuitive responses originate from joy and include:

◆ an instant recognition of a truth without knowing how you
know

◆ sensing that you are doing the right thing in making a choice
or decision even if it is not the immediately obvious option

◆ an experience of knowing the probable outcome just as it is
beginning to unfold

◆ sensing a purpose or a point to something without knowing
what it is.

## Definitions

The dictionary I looked at defines it as 'immediate unreasoned
perception'. Other names for intuitive experiences include:

◆ knowingness

◆ clairvoyance

◆ psychic ability

◆ common sense

◆ guardian angel

◆ spirit guide

◆ higher self

◆ wisdom

◆ collective unconscious

◆ déjà vu

◆ spiritual and emotional intelligence.

You will have your own reaction to each of these words, some
comfortable and some uncomfortable. These responses come
from your belief system, which affects your self-perception and
ability to trust your own intuition. Take a look at Exercise 2 at
the end of this chapter if you want to explore this point before
you go any further.

Once you are comfortable with what intuition means, you
can recognise the experiences you have. Intuition comes in
several forms:

- ◆ a sudden flash of insight, visual or auditory
- ◆ a predictive dream
- ◆ a spinal shiver of recognition as something is occurring or told to you
- ◆ a sense of knowing something already
- ◆ a snapshot image of a future scene or event
- ◆ knowledge, perspective or understanding divined from tools which respond to the subconscious mind
- ◆ the ability to see a bigger picture developing from small seemingly unconnected events.
- ◆ a deep sense of knowing and recognising yourself in all its dimensions
- ◆ recognising all the inner voices that influence your beliefs and choices in life.

It is all these and much more.

Intuition is an essential part of the whole experience of living. Although it will not help you predict the future or how other people will behave, using intuition as a guide makes life more rewarding. It helps you follow what seems to be the right path, even when social convention or common sense appears to indicate differently. Above all it teaches you how to trust yourself and to be your own best friend. The many ways in which intuition helps:

- ◆ It encourages a calm approach to life; to take chances, fear very little, and enjoy or accept everything as an experience.
- ◆ It enables you to interpret your emotions and recognise what they are telling you so that you can respond as you prefer.
- ◆ It helps you to make choices easily and without regrets.
- ◆ It helps you to accept what happens in life is for the best, even though it may not seem like that in the beginning.
- ◆ It is an approach to life which involves being able to trust yourself and be independent of other people and external influences.
- ◆ It is being internally referenced in how you live your life, what choices you make, how you respond to changes and generally living with the bigger picture perspective so that daily hassles stay firmly in proportion.
- ◆ It enables you to trust that you will be able to cope with whatever life throws at you and perceive everything as a positive experience.

- ◆ It allows you to take full responsibility for your own reality and experiences and live with a sense of your own truth.
- ◆ It is an infinitely versatile form of intelligence which is great fun and unrelated to education and academic achievement (did you know Einstein failed at school?).
- ◆ More than anything it helps you to be at peace with yourself and know that you have done your best in any situation and that making mistakes is part of developing greater understanding and intuitive ability.

Intuition is your trusted friend who is always at your shoulder. This friend knows and accepts everything there is to know about you, exactly how to deal with every situation as best as is possible and gives you an answer for every question when you are ready to hear and understand it. This friend will help you interpret all your experiences in the most positive way, enabling you to learn the most from them. It will guide you away from repeating mistakes and help you to make decisions when the most obvious, safe, logical choice may not be the best one.

## Denying intuitive experiences

We are all born with a degree of intuitive skill and ability and, according to childhood experience, we either develop this further or we may lose it, unaware of the value of what we have lost. For many children, 'older and wiser' adults who dismiss the knowingness of children as childhood fantasy deny their knowledge. As adults we may not have any recollection of these experiences or even be aware of how common they are. Such experiences include:

- ◆ having a sense of being able to fly at night
- ◆ having regular friends or persecutors in your dreams
- ◆ being aware of things out of the corner of your eye such as shadows, movements and colours that are not explained by normal means
- ◆ being aware of fairies, angels, ghosts or other spiritual and elemental beings
- ◆ being able to sense atmospheres or energies, and see colours around people

- being able to detect emotions and intentions in other people and have a sense of 'all is well/not well'
- being able to hear disembodied voices
- automatically and immediately liking or disliking someone without knowing why
- having a sense of otherness about yourself, aspects of yourself which seem to be missing in the present, to be somewhere else
- having a feeling of bonding with another time or place than where you lived as a child or live now
- feeling that so-called reality is an illusion and there is something else – seeing things shift form and then become solid again
- having a sense that everything is just perfect as it is.

And these are just a few! You could try Exercise 3 now or leave it until later.

## The power of words

There are several words which should be banned from common use because they preprogramme us to think in terms of failure and lead us away from our intuitive nature. The worst words are **try** and **why.**

- **Why** requires us to justify whatever we are doing or have done and can lead to withdrawal and guilt. We should never have to justify ourselves if we are comfortable with our choices in life. Challenges such as 'why do you want to do that' are really the other person stating that they would not want to or be able to do that and you are therefore making them feel uneasy about their limitations. Because they want to be right in their approach to life they will attempt to make you uncomfortable in yours. This is how we are manipulated into conformity.
- **Try** suggests that whatever effort you employ, you might not succeed. Success, progress, intelligence and learning are based on a thorough exploration of a subject or skill and must include all that works well and all that works less well. Whatever you do, you are doing it as best you can with what you know and can manage right now. You are always

doing it with varying degrees of mastery or skillfulness. Even people who set out to underachieve are doing so because they are unable to climb the two fearsome hurdles of failure and success; they are still doing the best they can with what they know in spite of their self-imposed emotional limitations.

So we can never try, we can either do or not do, there is nothing in between. And to create a 'trying zone' provides a let out clause so that you can justify avoiding success. There is no failure. There is just a process of trial and error, and of learning. All learning is positive even if it is learning how not to do things, because it allows you to know the differences. All learning leads to success, but it can do that much more effectively if we do not surround certain types of learning with fear based beliefs and reactions. Other limiting words are:

◆ should
◆ ought to
◆ could
◆ difficult
◆ but
◆ however
◆ limitation
◆ can't
◆ impossible
◆ lose/win/beat/wrong
◆ better/worse than someone else.

## Learning to succeed intuitively

Jerome Bruner, one of the most influential child psychologists, used the term 'scaffolding' to describe the support which surrounds a child learning basic motor and social skills such as language, walking etc. He saw that the support provided by caring people around the child enables him/her to keep practising until they achieve mastery of the skill. There is no failure, but a gradual increase in levels of competency and skillfulness.

> All rising to great places, is by a winding stair.
>
> (Francis Bacon)

Learning can only occur through direct and meaningful experience and is only complete when it is fully automatic and cannot be forgotten. You cannot forget something you fully know, or lose something you truly have mastered.

We cannot show a child how to hold a spoon and then expect them to do it immediately. The child can model their behaviour on the demonstration but then practise how it feels in their own hands through trial and error. Adopting this approach to all life experiences would benefit everyone throughout their lives, especially in their own emotional skill development. The irony is that we are often more able than we realise but it is our fear-based beliefs that stop us finding that out.

So really begin to acknowledge your intuitive experiences, all of them, even those you are not sure about for now. Even if you think it cannot be real remember that the science fiction stories of a few years ago are now more fact than fiction. The truth is we do not know what the limits are, so stop believing in them and let yourself open up to the probability that anything is possible. Whatever you imagine could become true for you and for anyone else too. Just let your imagination and your intuition lead you where it will and then sit back and let things happen in their own way – they will if you let them – it just takes a little time and our trust and patience is all that we need. Releasing the possibilities of your own potential is important. Don't decide on the future – let it show itself to you in its own way – then it just might be what your heart longs for. Just wait and see what happens next.

## Example

Children of aboriginal descent in Australia who still live in remote areas of the Australian outback live amongst lizards as part of the natural fauna of their lives. If a lizard loses its tail it can grow new ones. The children see this and believe in it. If they lose their finger or other small parts of their body, they also grow a new one, up until around five years of age. They believe they can do it and so it happens.

Medical science has filed this away as impossible because it breaks the rules and they do not know how to explain it in their own terms. The point is that these children do not know they cannot do this – so they can. Some species do this quite openly so why can't we? If our body has regenerative abilities anyway why can't they work in this way?

## Summary

- ◆ We can all develop intuition, it is a matter of choice.
- ◆ Intuition is always there and we can learn to tap into its resources within ourselves.
- ◆ Nothing is impossible except the ideas and beliefs we hold that tell us it is so.
- ◆ Thought creates reality.
- ◆ All of life is our learning ground for developing self awareness and intuition and we are all at different levels of mastery in different areas of experience.
- ◆ There is no such thing as a bad decision or failure, it is part of learning how to become more skilful.
- ◆ Keeping an open mind on everything allows us to explore and develop as individuals in ways which are limitless.

## Exercises

To make the most of the exercises in this book it is suggested that you keep a diary of your development and responses. This becomes a rich resource for you to use whenever you are feeling stuck in the future, and a reminder of how far you have already travelled.

### Exercise 1. Keeping a diary

To enhance your progress and use every day's experiences to their maximum, keep a diary as a record of your progress. This is both to enable you to work steadily through the exercises in each chapter, and to acknowledge how intuitive you are becoming.

Also writing around three sides of paper each morning as you first begin the day is a good way of clearing your mind and leaving it open and receptive to new intuitions as they arise after a good night's sleep. Just write automatically whatever comes to your thoughts as you discharge their energy and free-up yourself. Most importantly do not try and craft anything, do not imagine that anyone is ever going to read these notes – they are just for you to work with for yourself. Honesty comes straight from the heart and mind without refinement by our self conscious inner judge. If you want be develop your intuition you must get to know yourself at much deeper levels, your motivations and fears, your hurts and beliefs, your hopes and joy.

## Exercise 2

Ask yourself the following questions and write down your responses.

◆ What does intuition mean to you?

◆ In what way do you think intuition will be useful to you or used by you to improve the quality of your life?

◆ What experiences have you had that you would describe as intuitive?

◆ What experiences have you had that struck you as coincidences but that you dismissed and put down to chance?

## Exercise 3

Make a note of which words in this chapter that you find most comfortable to work with. Now ask yourself if it matters which are used if they all ask more or less the same thing. Think about what makes some words uncomfortable for you. Make notes here and explore your own thinking and beliefs. There is no right or wrong, this is purely what *you* think and feel now.

## Exercise 4

Spend a few moments remembering if any of the experiences you have read about in this chapter were familiar to you or seemed to rekindle some sort of memory. Do not worry if you cannot remember anything from this list or anything at all similar. This does not mean that you are not intuitive or did not have intuitive experiences as a child, but that the experiences are buried deep or went unrecognised at the time. Some time after reading this exercise, you may find memories and thoughts returning. It is a good idea to keep a record of these experiences in your diary. Once you realise how intuitive you are you will begin to become far more aware of other experiences happening all the time and your mind will become more open and receptive to noticing intuitive experiences.

CHAPTER 2

# Connecting Intelligence and Intuition

As we began to establish in Chapter 1, intuition and imagination are forms of intelligence, higher intelligence than intellect or knowledge acquisition. That is an opinion of course, but one supported by some very intelligent people.

> When I examine myself and my methods of thought, I come to the conclusion that the gift of fantasy has meant more to me than my talent for absorbing positive knowledge.
>
> (Albert Einstein)

Intuition is a form of intelligence that is infinitely versatile and not related to education or academic achievement. The word intelligence means ability to understand, reason and perceive – mental alertness. Intuition fits the bill perfectly in terms of being all the above. It allows us:

◆ to see things in alternative perspectives, i.e. subjective, hypothetical, surreal

◆ to recognise and value perceptions that do not fit with the rational mind, i.e. to understand without knowing why we understand

◆ to be mentally alert to the truths that lie beneath our superficial perceptions and rational explanations for experience i.e. hidden agendas and dishonesty

◆ to accept reasons for things in life that have no rational reason other than they just are that way, i.e. synchronicity or coincidences and the unexpected twist and turns of life paths.

Intuition is certainly one of the most important aspects of overall intelligence. But this is not what we usually think of when we use the term intelligence in our present culture. This chapter explores concepts of intelligence, how it is influenced by social beliefs and culture, and why certain types of intelligence are regarded with caution or even fear or rejection. By understanding more about how intuition works we can begin to understand how intuition fits into the picture of human experience and why intuitive self awareness is more important than academic achievement, although both play important roles in our lives.

## Arriving with intuitive skills

We all unconsciously recognise and identify more about a person than what is superficially obvious. Some of this is from our own pre-suppositions and stereotypes. But there is another layer of recognition that goes far deeper, which sees the agendas and unconscious beliefs in somebody, senses their emotional makeup and/or dispositions of behaviour and intention, their neediness and the games they use to extract the needs from others.

Children are born with strong intuitive abilities. It is the basis for their survival. It is also essential for interpersonal and social skills to develop in a positive and useful way. Common examples of this are:

◆ Children are frequently more accurate than adults in assessing the intentions and underlying emotions in other people. Their uneasiness with certain people is then chastised for causing embarrassment to the adults around and they begin to lose touch or distrust their intuitive understandings.

◆ They often report seeing beings or having experiences and dreams that far outstrip the rational explanations that adults try to place upon them. So they are labelled childish imagination.

◆ Sometimes they appear quite irrational in their like or dislike for certain people, to the point of distress and crying when meeting certain people and yet are proved correct later on when behaviour patterns betray the intentions and emotional make up of these same individuals.

Sometimes this ability, this intuitive knowledge, is explained as reading non-verbal communication, NVC for short. But there is usually more to it than can be psychologically measured or explained as NVC. This is intuition, a 'knowing' that can only be experienced subjectively, often with a strong emotional experience attached. And even if it were NVC, how are young children so much more able to read it than some adults?

## Measuring intuition

We cannot measure or assess intuition because we cannot see it. For the last couple of centuries we have followed the empirical line in all research, i.e. if it cannot be observed and measured it does not exist. This is the basis for a general rejection or dismissal and undervaluing of intuition as a real force for change, a real intelligence. Hence the dismissal of children's experiences which challenge this model as purely childish and not to be taken seriously.

However, it is possible to measure outcomes. Just as we cannot visually see electricity, we know it runs through wires and we can see the outcomes, i.e. lights glow and appliances work for us. But no one has ever actually seen electricity in its raw state. Research does show that intuition is far more accurate in, for instance, medical diagnosis than just using symptoms as a guidance mechanism.

In some ways medical intuition is easy to measure because you have a presenting set of symptoms by which you can check the diagnosis of the intuitive. This offers a direct measurement of accuracy in intuitive diagnosis without any knowledge of the client other than perhaps name and age. One of the most famous intuitives of the twentieth century was Edgar Cayce. He not only gave accurate diagnosis of illness but also gave the psycho/spiritual basis behind the illness that was being experienced. His suggestions gave a great deal of insight into the nature of illness and enabled many people to heal themselves.

In the latter part of the twentieth century another medical intuitive, Dr Caroline Myss, undertook some tests in a research project where she was given only the patient's name and date of birth. She was 93 per cent accurate in a correct diagnosis for each patient. That is far higher than any doctor's medical accuracy even with full medical information and case notes.

We will look at a lot more research into intuitive experiences later in this book. But this statistic alone must make you think that there is far more than can be rationally explained by present models of understanding.

## Subjective experiences

One of the problems our society has with intuition is that it is a subjective experience. This means that we cannot rationally explain it or measure it as it occurs. When outcomes are measured, alternative explanations are often sought, rather than an acceptance of non-rational explanations such as intuition. Subjective experience is viewed as unreliable data for most psychological research. However humanistic and other forms of modern psychology like NLP (neurolinguistic programming) do accept the validity of subjective experience in terms of its reality for the individual. The aim is not to seek an explanation of why something works, just to accept that it does and how to model and reproduce it. NLP accepts that anything is possible and limitation arises only from belief.

### Case Study: Mark knows

Mark was 3 years old when his parents separated. Four years later his mother Anna met Mike. Mark immediately distrusted Mike even though there was nothing outwardly wrong with his behaviour. When he tried to tell Anna his feelings, he was told not to be jealous, which he was not. He loved his mother and wanted her to be happy, but there was something wrong. Mark did his best to live with Mike but was increasingly unhappy. He began to feel that his 'jealousy' was blamed for everything and even Anna began to tell him how difficult he had become. After a couple of years Mike began to treat Anna increasingly unkindly but Mark was still blamed for the difficulties when it was clearly Mike who now caused the tension.

Although Mark was doing his best to cope with things at home, he was also having problems at school. Mark found it hard to sit still and learn in the way that other children did in his class. He liked to feel things, to take them apart and explore them in all sorts of ways of his own. He felt quite excited at all the new possibilities for learning and exploring that school seemed to offer him, but his teacher told him to sit down all the time. His frustration grew daily and he found it hard to learn anything. He found that the only lessons he could relate to were drama, art and music. He attracted praise for his artwork from the other children too and found he could make them laugh through his pictures and sense of humour. Gradually he found he had a real talent for making the other children laugh in class and found all sorts of opportunities for turning any situation into an opportunity for him to excel at what he could do best. He became very popular with the other children and felt that the label of being 'the naughty boy' was worth the social popularity and success he now experienced. Letters went home from school and Anna punished him for letting himself down. This was a blow to Mark who now lost a great deal of self-esteem. He felt trapped between the only success he found he could achieve and being told he was a bad person for exploring this social success with his peers. And his mother was now rejecting him even more.

Eventually Mike went too far and Anna saw what Mark had seen all along. She became clairvoyant i.e. clear sighted and recognised the games that Mike had been playing with her and with Mark. Mark was pleased when Mike left and relieved that he had been right all along. His self-esteem returned somewhat and Anna's and Mark's relationship improved at home at least. But school was still a problem. _____

## Denying intuitive realities

We assume that we as adults know more than our children, but in reality, they often see more clearly than adults because their thoughts are not cluttered with hidden agendas, justifications and excuses. These attitudes are called ego blocks (see Chapter 11). They separate us from our own truths out of fear. Society compounds this by sending children to schools which teach that intuitive thought and experience is not a valid way of working, and that only linear thought and logical reasoning is worthwhile. This is slowly changing.

Achievement is measured in these terms and other types of intelligence are labelled as being dysfunctional. This is especially true of dyslexia, attention deficit disorder (ADD) and other 'educational learning difficulties'.

Mark's learning approach is kinaesthetic and intuitive. He cannot sit still and listen, he needs to explore and learn through all his senses. He has great intuition about how to be popular with other people and make them laugh and feel joy.

This is not valued by authority figures. Mark is a very intelligent child but he cannot demonstrate this at school. He can only show it 'as he is' and this is labelled as unacceptable.

> I am enough of an artist to draw freely upon my imagination. Imagination is more important than knowledge. Knowledge is limited. Imagination encircles the world.
>
> (Albert Einstein, 1929)

## The seven kinds of intelligence

Howard Gardner (1983) identifies seven kinds of intelligence:

1  Language-based skill, the ability to use words and listening skills.
2  Social or interpersonal intelligence; the ability to get along with people wherever and whoever they are.
3  Self-motivational intelligence, the ability to be self-directed and self motivated.

These first three go to make up emotional intelligence. This was summarised very well by Daniel Goleman in his book of the same name and has generated a new interest in this approach to intelligence that is being promoted in some areas of education at present. Then there is:

4  Logical linear intelligence used in things like sequential maths and scientific approaches, to follow logic and straight lines of reasoning.

In Western society, this is most commonly understood to represent intelligence in its entirety, together with language skills, but with snippets of the following included, which are:

5  Spatial skills and the ability to visualise and manipulate mental images.
6  Musical intelligence and the ability to respond and experience music, to play music creatively and spontaneously rather than the processed linear approach taught by most music teachers.
7  Body 'kinaesthetic' intelligence; the ability to move athletically; fine motor skills; coordination between hand,

eye and other body parts; creative and artistic skills and crafts.

So how gifted is the musician who cannot read or write music but can play songs, who has never passed a music exam in their life but can transport people with their intuitive understanding of harmonies and chord sequences? How talented is an artist who has never been to art college but can create wonderful images from clay or paint? How talented is the writer or poet who has not passed English exams but can captivate a reader with their words. And acrobats, contortionists, and athletes who have never studied sports science but can make their body work in wonderful ways. And gardeners, and builders, and anyone who has ever had a dream. The list is endless.

> We should take care not to make the intellect our God; it has, of course, powerful muscles but no personality.
>
> (Albert Einstein)

## Spiritual intelligence

Even more recently, an eighth approach to intelligence has been identified as spiritual intelligence. That is people who have a sense of their own spiritual nature beyond the religious, orthodox, rule- and ritual-following. This shows itself in people's ability to cope with the ups and downs of life more or less successfully and the inclination towards depression breakdowns and self-pity/victimhood. This is an old tradition and was well documented by Rudolph Steiner and more recently Michael Levin.

## Intuitive intelligence

I would put intuitive intelligence above all the listed classifications simply because it includes them all but with the added power of being able to recognise which one is being used and to move through all of them without needing to stop and think about it. To know without knowing why we know. In other words, it is a holistic approach to intelligence which excludes nothing and no one. It positively embraces the right to learn through mistakes and without fear of shame for being 'wrong' because you cannot be wrong to learn from experience. And we have Einstein's agreement on that.

## So how do we know what intelligence is?

When we start to recognise different kinds of intelligence and apply them to people, it paints a very different picture. But whatever style of learning we prefer, we have to learn from personal experience to truly know something for ourselves. Thus experimentation and making mistakes is the only way to really learn anything – and that takes courage in a society which punishes mistakes and criticises divergent approaches to life.

> The only source of knowledge is personal experience.
> (Albert Einstein)

So think about Mark in the case study and decide:
- Which kinds of intelligence is Mark demonstrating?
- Are his needs being recognised and nurtured at home or at school?
- How will this teach Mark to value his ways of expressing himself and his approach to life?

Study the exercise at the end of this chapter if you want to explore your own intelligence.

## Ways of knowing

Gardner points out that almost all present educational experiences are based on language and linear intelligence. Our education system is based on packing a child full of knowledge that is often irrelevant to their actual experiences of life at that point. And we authoritatively tell them that they need this information for their future or they will fail in life. They are judged and classified from an early age.

> Whoever undertakes to set himself up as a judge in the field of truth and knowledge is shipwrecked by the laughter of the Gods.
>
> (Albert Einstein)

Skills in the other areas are even classified as behavioural disorders or learning difficulties. A person who is very kinaesthetically intelligent may have difficulty in staying in one place for long, wanting to touch things and move around in order to experience and learn. This is commonly called disruptive behaviour or given a label such as ADD, which teaches us not to trust our innate and intuitive ways of learning. Yet these are the ways that our intuition will lead us and teach us all we really need to learn in life.

Everyone has his or her own way of knowing. The alternative forms of intelligence are exactly the skills you will develop as you work through this book. You will develop a much closer relationship with your inner tutor and find your true intelligence, based on your intuition.

## Energising thoughts

A thought creates reality. In psychological terms this refers to the self-fulfilling prophecy theory. But is this all it is?

All brain activities result in firing a neural pathway through the brain. The firing is a charge of electrical current that passes along the neuron, causing a release of neurotransmitters into the next connecting neuron. Thus information gets passed around the entire nervous system. All electrical current creates an energy field (people who live near pylons for example have health problems related to these energy fields). Every single thought activity in the brain releases this current which in turn creates a field around it. What happens to this energy field? It radiates outward through our skulls and into the universe as a very light form of energy vibration. We can sometimes feel people's thought fields if they have a strong energy behind them – like love or anger.

All energy is creative, vibrates at differing resonances, and transmutes form continuously – a basic scientific principle. Energy cannot be created or destroyed, and it is the basis for all that exists. So thoughts become realities through their energy fields transmuting one form into another. Stick with this idea as it develops throughout the book. Energy and brain activity are where intuition, physics, biology, maths and cosmology all meet.

> The important thing is not to stop questioning. Curiosity
> has its own reason for existing. One cannot help but be in
> awe when he contemplates the mysteries of eternity, of the
> marvellous structure of reality. It is enough if one merely
> tries to comprehend a little of this mystery every day.
> Never lose a holy curiosity.
>
> (Albert Einstein)

## Recognising brain styles

Different kinds of intelligence are also related to different brain
styles. The brain can be sub-divided in many ways and
different parts of the brain fulfil different but interrelated
functions. Evidence supporting the concept that different parts
of the brain operate in different ways was first demonstrated by
Sperry through work he carried out with people who
underwent a section (cutting) of the *corpus callosum* in order
to control extreme and life-threatening epilepsy (Figure 1).
Sperry conducted numerous tests on how these people
functioned and noted several differences. The most significant
evidence demonstrated that:

◆ different halves of the cerebral cortex have different
   functions

◆ the right brain seemed to have limited functions and mostly
   supported the left side

◆ the left side dominated the right side of the body and was
   principally connected with language and logical, sequential
   thinking.

For a time the left side became known as the dominant brain.
More recent research which followed this early finding has
shown further, more hierarchical divisions of the brain.

## Introducing models of three

A model of functional and regional division identified by Dr P.
Maclean was called the triune brain. Based on the brain
structure in Figure 1, he calls the brain stem and cerebellum
the reptilian brain, with the limbic system and cerebral cortex
both developing later and serving sequentially higher functions

as humans evolved. Each part became responsible for different functions according to levels of mental awareness and cognitive needs of the human species. Evolution occurred as a result of intelligence, not the other way round, as commonly supposed.

(a) The reptilian brain governs basic physical survival. It forms patterns of behaviour, routines, habits and instinctive behaviour such as survival needs of food, shelter and reproduction. This relates mostly to the body.

(b) The limbic system is a chemically active region of the brain and responds most to the neurotransmitters, the chemical messengers of the nervous system throughout the entire body. It is the origin of most emotions and immediate emotional responses such as fight or flight, fear/self-protection. This relates to the emotions.

(c) The neo-cortex is divided into left and right. It is to do with all the logical, analytical, linguistic aspects of humanity (left brain), as well as all the creative, imaginative and intuitive aspects of being human (right brain). This relates to knowledge and enlightenment.

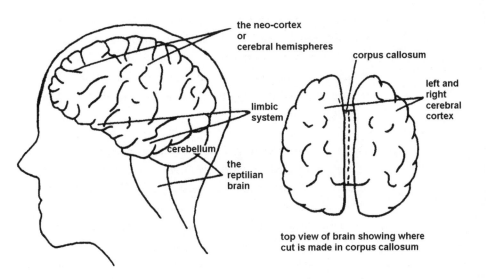

Fig. 1. The triune brain.

Another researcher, Herrmann, sees this as still only part of the story. Based on the work of Sperry, he suggested left and right subdivisions of the limbic system and the neo-cortex, and identified different regions of the brain as a quadrant of upper and lower left, and upper and lower right brains, with the reptilian brain taking care of automatic functions. By using tests and electrodes to measure brain activity, Herrmann was further able to subdivide the upper and mid regions of the brain into four areas associated with specific functions.

◆ Upper left (cerebral cortex). Includes the scientific approach, mathematical and logical procedural thinking styles, problem solving on a step-by-step basis, linear thinking.

◆ Lower left (limbic system). The planner and organiser role, controls and administers approaches to life and living.

◆ Upper right (cerebral cortex). Capable of seeing the whole picture, intuitive and artistic, endlessly creative and innovative.

◆ Lower right (limbic system). The emotional brain responds to people, music and creative stimuli; the talker and interpersonal brain.

By thus dividing up brain functions, Herrmann was able to measure people's brain styles and see which quadrant they functioned from most. These are his conclusions:

◆ intuitive functions originate from right brain dominance
◆ conventional teaching measures and values only left brain dominance.

This confirms the strongly cultural bias in western society. Other cultures, which work intuitively, are able to function intuitively as part of normal everyday experience. Children in these cultures are encouraged to develop these skills as a normal part of their learning. Jamie Sams points out that the child born with natural psychic (called shamanic) talents in native American cultures is supported in learning to 'walk with them', in the belief that lack of support will lead to mental illness and schizophrenia through an inability to know which inner voices to listen to, which to ignore and how to manage them.

## *Intuition and anatomy*

However, avoiding a classical reductionist approach, intuition should not be defined as a purely anatomical ability, only available to right brain dominated people or those from certain cultures. In working with many hundreds of individuals, I have noticed how much we all differ in where we store information. Different parts of our understanding of the same incident can come from different areas of the brain. This is most clearly noted by watching eyes when people are asked to recall something, but in some cases I get clients to point to the different directions that information is coming from. This is a basic NLP approach to being able to recognise and recreate excellence.

## Appreciating the potential of intuition

Intuition is one of the most powerful tools life offers because it combines all dimensions of the brain. It is working on the bigger picture. It can see how things will work through. It allows for ups and downs in that process. Emotional intelligence is now recognised as a key component of true intuition. It is increasingly recognised as the true basis of personal success and social problem sorting. It is accepted as essential for business success and is included in business management degree courses. Senior executives are even given 'intuition time allowances' in their contracts and terms of working conditions.

> Intuition directs us to the best choices we can make. Emotional intelligence recognises our choices and understands why we think and feel as we do, learning the lessons each choice offers.

**Case Study: Confusion**

At a crossroads in his life, Peter was faced with gloomy prospects of a safe and ultimately very limited life, or to take a chance now and find out what could happen next. His relationship had broken down, his company was asking for redundancies with a good package and he felt generally frustrated with his whole life. When asked to locate all these different thoughts and considerations, he found that each one was situated in a different part of his mind. He drew a map of where each part was located then played around to see how it felt to move them around, to experiment with the perceptual outcomes of each choice. Finally, using hypnosis as a tool, he was guided into each option and his subconscious mind was asked to look at only positive outcomes for each aspect of his 'mind'. These aspects were invited to sort it out between them. The following week his intuition had come up with the answer and he knew exactly what he wanted to do. He took the redundancy and started his own firm as a freelance designer. He stepped into his new life choice with confidence and never looked back. _____

## Summary

Using the whole brain means recognising all the influences and aspects of how your brain works.

- ◆ In most people intuitive functions can be located in the right brain which is associated with creativity and 'whole picture' perceptions of life.
- ◆ It is important to recognise that beliefs and attitudes towards intuition are largely culturally and socially based and can therefore be usefully questioned.
- ◆ We can choose from many models, words and approaches to develop the same skills.
- ◆ Everyone is an individual, their own experiences and understanding are right for them, so there are no rights or wrongs.

## Exercises

### *Exercise 1*

Again use your diary for this work as a record of your thoughts and feelings. It will help you to recognise your beliefs and make decisions to change them.

Look at the areas of intelligence discussed in this chapter and consider how these relate to you.

- ◆ How much have you valued yourself in these terms?
- ◆ How much have you felt yourself to be inadequate in these terms?

- How much are you willing to re-examine yourself and your sense of self worth now in light of these ideas?

The more you are willing to explore the beliefs you have held about life up to this point, the more you will be able to find your true potential.

## Exercise 2

This is best done with a friend and you can take it in turns to help each other to explore your brain map. Ask the following questions and note where people look for the answers.

1  If you could choose wherever you wanted to go on holiday, where would you choose?
2  What does your car look like?
3  What did you wear the last time you went out to a party?
4  Who else was at this party?
5  How did you enjoy this party?
6  What will you be doing this time next week?
7  Think of something that makes you very happy.
8  Think of something that makes you sad or angry or both.

What you should find, if you are both relaxed, is that your partner's eyes went in different directions for each bit of information, especially where you asked for different bits of information for the same event. Each person will be different and there is no right or wrong way to experience this, you are just exploring.

*The only true experience is of the immediate present, to its fullest depth.*

# Becoming Acquainted with the Intuitive Self

To become more acquainted with the intuitive self means becoming more self-aware. Most of the time we live on the surface of our experiences, with a complex mix of past and future issues competing for our attention. All of these cloud the full potential of the present moment. To really find our intuitive self we have to go deeper into the present moment, and learn to listen to our inner voices, to recognise where they come from and to understand which ones to follow. That, it seems, is the scary part for most people because we have been taught to trust only what we can measure and test according to Cartesian, scientific, empirical principles.

> Few are those who see with their own eyes and feel with their own hearts.
>
> (Albert Einstein)

So how can we hear the quiet voice of intuition with this cacophony going on in our minds all the time? Most of us are using our intuition regularly but are unaware of what is really occurring. The prevailing attitude in our society is that attempting to develop greater self-understanding is a need to 'sort yourself out' and indicates emotional 'problems' to be ashamed of. Therefore most people in western society are remarkably unself-aware. In addition, the speed and level of external stimulus we are subject to make it increasingly difficult to know what is going on inside and how we are responding. The subconscious mind processes millions of bits of information every second. How much of this are you aware of?

> The most beautiful thing we can experience is the mysterious. It is the source of all true art and science. He to whom this emotion is a stranger, who can no longer pause to wonder and stand rapt in awe, is as good as dead: his eyes are closed.
>
> (Albert Einstein)

## Responding instinctively

Young children are completely instinctive in their approach to life. They prefer to eat and sleep when their body needs to. As parents and adults we train them into routines, i.e. to change their response from their own body rhythms to a routine convenient for society. Some parents will know how hard this is, as some children are very strongly based in their own patterns and rhythms. This establishes a basis of conflict for parents and the beginnings of labelling a child 'difficult'.

Children live in the immediate present and enjoy each moment for what it holds. As western adults we have lost this ability because we are taught not to trust it. We are taught to think of the past and the future in a way which over-emphasises their importance. Yet the only true experience is of the immediate present. The past is over and the future is endless in its possibilities, but it hasn't happened yet.

### *Experiencing the present*

Many belief systems teach that staying present or being 'mindful' is the basic principle behind inner peace and contentment. Being mindful means giving your full concentration to whatever you are doing in the present, having no real awareness of anything else, becoming completely absorbed, lost in the activity and the moment. This experience of the moment means we are far more likely to notice things around us, clues and insights we miss when future and past are mixed with the present. We are also less aware of how we are feeling if we are not present.

> Becoming fully aware of our feelings and emotions is a very powerful aspect of developing intuition.

Living in the moment is the only way to remain happy in your life, to be:

◆ contented, fulfilled and relaxed
◆ living with a sense of peace and calm
◆ in tune with your own body
◆ not feeling obliged to respond or react to other people's behaviour
◆ reading the signals from your nervous system and relating them to the ideas and images in your mind
◆ responsible for your own experiences in life
◆ finding enjoyment in all that your life holds.

**Try it now**    Is the list above how you would define happiness or contentment? How else might you describe and experience happiness? Think what happiness really means for you. Close your eyes and remember a time when you knew you were truly happy. As you run through the experience again, notice the components of your happiness. What makes this experience noticeably happy in your mind? As you find out what happiness means to you, make notes of this in your diary.

## Taking responsibility

We often think of life as something that happens to us. When we live intuitively we find that life happens *within* and *from* us. What is the difference? It is the difference between confusion and contentment.

If we feel confusion, we usually want to find a reason. We say:

◆ this has happened in the past and still affects me
◆ that might happen some time ahead and I have to be cautious
◆ I am uncertain what is happening and I don't know what to do.

These kinds of feelings cannot occur in the present. We are so busy living in the past or the future that the present becomes an unfamiliar experience and we waste it or feel uncomfortable in it. Then we start finding external reasons for this discomfort, something out there to blame it all on. Common examples are:

- I went to a bad school/poor teachers/unrecognised talents
- I had abusive/critical/unaware parents
- the social and economic conditions were/are too hard for me
- previous experience only confirms that...
- other people behave badly towards me
- no one understands me.

All of these are victim attitudes, based on the idea that things happen to us and we have no control over them.

## Recognising our patterns

Most of us hold this kind of attitude in some form or another. Yet if difficult experiences continue to happen to some people and not others, that suggests a pattern or a common denominator, not chance. Once we can recognise our own patterns, we will still have ups and downs in life but the downs are never so low or long and the ups are more exciting with endless possibilities. This is the key difference to living intuitively.

- There is only one way to make life more comfortable and that is to look at how you respond to life.
- By becoming more acquainted with how you think about and experience life, you can start to relax and take more of an overview perspective of situations, see them for what they are and respond accordingly.
- By seeing the big picture and becoming more responsible for your own life experiences, you can start to experience your own life in a simpler and more honest way.

We can only do this by becoming acquainted with the inner, intuitive self. As we increasingly understand our reactions and emotional responses, we develop a deeper sense of self which enables a calmer, richer daily experience of life. Try Exercise 2 now or later on.

## Understanding the subconscious mind

The subconscious mind is still largely a mystery to psychologists. As Schachter states, if the human brain could be completely understood, humans would not have the ability to even recognise the existence of a brain. It is often a case of the more we discover, the more we realise there is still to understand.

Even with limited understanding we are reasonably certain of some things it can do. The subconscious mind has learned to work in visual patterns, based on experience. The limbic system has learned to respond emotionally, again based on experience. Together they serve to guide us and protect us through life. That is their function and sole purpose. There are two basic perceptual positions which develop:

(a) fear/mistrust-based perceptions

(b) joyful/trust-based perceptions.

Most people are a mixture of both but each of us will have a dominance in one. Western society is based on fear. Living intuitively teaches us to live with joy.

This has several consequences:

♦ A brain system based on fear will distrust anything that is not tried, tested and proved, including intuitive thinking.

♦ People who live with a fear bias believe that everything will be OK as long as nothing changes.

♦ Fear wants to keep controlled routines, nothing spontaneous, so everyone knows what to expect.

### The effect of living with fear

People living with any of these beliefs dominating their lives are immediately limited. Thinking patterns based on fear are resistant to change, challenges and opportunities. Life can never be as much fun as it should be. Fear attitudes are perpetuated by logical thinking processes and diminished by intuitive living.

> We poison our lives with fear of burglary and shipwreck, and ask anyone, the house is never burgled and the ship never goes down.
>
> (Jean Anouilh)

It appears, from brain scan evidence, that intuitive 'thinking', or perception, comes from the right brain and is based on the ability to see the bigger 'holistic' picture rather than to focus on individual experiences. This also enables us to see how things are connected to each other and nothing is 'out of the blue'. This is a basis for belief in Karma and our personal agency in our own life. We create our own experiences and outcomes by our actions and beliefs.

Intuitive living encompasses change as part of the natural order of things and even as something exciting and challenging, an opportunity. It tends to avoid rigid routine and prefers to live spontaneously. So living intuitively is not limiting and is not based on fear of what might happen.

> Life is ours to be spent, not to be saved.
>                                          (D H Lawrence)

The intuitive approach to life also likes to work with metaphor as a way of interpreting the 'bigger picture', because sometimes we just can't 'see' it any other way. Dreams are often metaphors for the events occurring in our waking lives. Sometimes they are telling us to look again to see things for what they really are – to look beneath the surface and to be honest with ourself. They help us to face our fears and recognise the challenges we prefer to avoid and hide from. Both Jung and Freud explored dreams as a key to understanding and accessing the unconscious mind and finding out more about who we are at a deeper level. We come to this later on but if you want to explore dreams now go to Exercise 3.

## Responding to natural rhythms

Dreams occur as part of natural rhythms of sleep. Daydreams occur as part of natural waking rhythms. Dreams always leave a perception of distorted time. Psychological research has identified the existence of rhythms or cycles that affect different parts of the human experience, especially our dream states. These are closely related to an experience of time passing and affect different people in different ways. We often have to modify our perceptions of time as we live intuitively because we respond more naturally to our bodies in relation to the seasons of the year. Becoming more self-aware means becoming acquainted with these rhythms.

## Noticing rhythms in time

One step in changing our perceptions of time is to recognise that time does not move in straight lines of past, present, future. There are cycles or seasons, like night and day and the seasons of the year. Some people react to different amounts of daylight and need more or less sleep during summer and winter, or feel more or less alive and connected.

Our body also responds in cycles or rhythms. There are several specific rhythms affecting all humans through each 24-hour period: the circadian, the diurnal and the ultradian rhythms.

## The circadian rhythm

Circadian, from Latin *circa dies*, means 'about one day' This rhythm charts the changes in our physiology and body chemistry over a 24-hour period. Our body responds to the release of certain hormones and body chemicals which make us feel sleepy at certain times and awake at others. These are released from part of the brain which is photosensitive, i.e. it responds to light. So we also feel the need for less sleep in the lighter parts of the year and more in the darker months. Sensitivity to this system is the cause of SAD, seasonal affective disorder. Some people become depressed during the darker months and therapy consists of sitting in front of powerful artificial light sources. It also affects people who work in buildings with poor lighting and little opportunity of experiencing natural daylight.

We are synchronised to rhythms, and light and dark affect breathing, blood and heart rates, metabolic rates and body temperature. Most commonly these functions reach a peak during the late morning/midday, and a lull during the middle hours of the night. This rhythm is internally controlled but externally triggered so changes to routines and patterns cause stress, i.e. change which takes time adjusting to. Shift workers and night workers have to change their circadian rhythm to suit a different pattern. The pattern does not matter but the consistency of it does. It is also the basis of jet lag.

## Levels of arousal

Levels of arousal are linked to the circadian rhythm, so we are more and less alert at different times of the day. There are different types of alertness change:

- ◆ Tonic changes are between sleep and wakefulness and the various levels which occur throughout a day.
- ◆ Phasic changes happen in response to stimuli like sudden interruptions or sudden demands upon us.

## The diurnal rhythms

Notice when you feel more or less alert during the day. These are tonic changes and are a response to **diurnal rhythms**. Thus, we have periods of more or less activity. It is quite common to have a slump time in mid-afternoon. This is caused by changes in brain activity and has several symptoms to identify it. Not everybody experiences this to the same degree but everyone will have it. This is the best time to relax for 15–20 minutes. You will clear your mind of the chemicals involved in the process and allow your body to re-adjust itself. After that you become more alert than if you struggle through it and fight against the brain chemical changes taking place, holding them up and making yourself less effective in the long run. It also has the effect of making you feel bad and, sometimes, headachy and irritable.

## Phasic alertness

Phasic alertness is your ability to suddenly respond with different speeds to different stimuli. Some things require urgent, fast responses for safety reasons. We often place non-urgent things into this response style and cause ourselves unnecessary stress. This originates from a fear of reprisal or criticism. Most of life can be dealt with at a leisurely pace and the outcome will be just as effective. Phasic alertness also affects breathing and heart rates, and causes tensing of muscles and pupil dilation. These are adverse physiological effects and can lead to long-term illness related to stress and an undermining of the immune system. During any hour your phasic alertness levels can change many times and during a day your tonic alertness will follow a pattern.

## The ultradian rhythm

Finally the ultradian rhythm affects us in 90-minute cycles during both day and night. It is related to stages of sleep and dreaming at night, but during the day to feelings of tonic alertness, i.e. you will feel more or less alert in roughly 90-minute cycles. You normally wake at the beginning of a cycle, especially if you wake at the same time each day without or just before the alarm goes. You can use this as a rough measurement of ultradian cycles. The afternoon slump is also a stage in this ultradian rhythm. If you feel like having a brain slump, give in to it, as much as you can and as often as you can. This is your right brain taking over for a while and you will be most receptive to intuitive experiences. Allow yourself to drift and see where your unconscious mind takes you. Not only will you benefit from opening your intuitive mind up, but you will work more efficiently when you resume a more alert part of the cycle.

## The power hour

The concept of a power hour is common to many cultures and is usually 23 hours opposite your slump time. So if you slump at 4 p.m. your power hour is probably at 4 a.m. Because we are so completely locked into the 24-hour clock we are mostly unaware of our power hours and sleep through them. Because we have set working times, we are usually unable to follow our body rhythms, yet this system enables us to get the most out of ourselves with the least distress. So by tracking our natural rhythms we will become more effective and less stressed.

## Learning balance

It is not practical for most people to take time out during the day to slump and switch into their intuition. There are, however, other ways in which you can balance both halves of your brain. One of the best ways is through breathing. Although, as mentioned earlier, each half of the body is controlled by the opposite half of the brain, this applies only to from immediately below the eyes down. The eyes themselves are split into a left and a right visual field, so each eye is controlled by both halves of the brain. The nose, however, is the nearest part of the body to the brain which is split in dominance. Each nostril is controlled by a different half of the brain, so most people have a dominant nostril through which they breathe. This too can be an indication of which side of the brain normally dominates.

## Defining clairvoyance and clairaudience

Intuition can be experienced by seeing the big picture, using the imagination constructively as a creative device. Imagination is the greatest tool we have as humans. Nothing we have achieved as a species could have occurred without someone first imagining it as a possibility.

> A personal daily mantra is a reminder of creative imagination: *Thought creates reality – therefore my thoughts create my reality.*

This has several benefits.

(a) It reminds you to keep in the present, to deal with what comes up and *actually* happens, not to run off into imaginary futures and panic.

(b) Whatever you think for the future is likely to become your reality, so you must keep your imagination positive and create in a responsible way – responsible to yourself.

(c) It reminds you to keep aware of your thoughts and to monitor them to stay positive and open to living.

(d) It reminds you that you alone can take responsibility for your own life, to blame no one and make no excuses.

(e) You can learn from experience and you can make mistakes as part of that learning.

(f) If you want an adventurous life you must first imagine it, then allow it to happen. Remain open to the developments as they unfold each day and trust your ability to deal with whatever comes up.

## Clairvoyance

The ability to 'see' this knowledge is called clairvoyance, i.e. seeing clearly what to do, think, feel or say next. This ability is linked to the brow *chakra* (see Chapter 10) and can come in several ways:

◆ Sometimes we can actually see the picture in our imagination, and it can arrive quite clearly and of its own accord.

◆ The experiences often appear as a short 'movie' on an internal screen.

◆ They are events in the future but you experience them as if they are happening right now.

◆ Sometimes you feel and even smell, hear and taste these insights.

◆ Sometimes the image can be fleeting and indistinct, so easily overlooked if not caught by a practiced intuitive.

## Clairaudience

Clairaudience comes with the ability to communicate clearly. If you can express yourself honestly and openly, then you can also *hear* openly and honestly. This is more difficult to balance and control because we have all sorts of inner voices which can seem to be clairaudience but are not. Clairaudience requires you to hush the chatter, clear your mind and *listen*. Both clairvoyance and clairaudience require time and silence, the ability to be in the present and to notice experiences that come to you.

## Having lots of fun

One of the most important things to remember with intuition is that it is fun: enormous, hilarious, adventurous, creative fun. Like a young child, living intuitively makes the world full of adventures waiting to happen, so get out there and start exploring. If you approach this self-development work with any other attitude your efforts will be counterproductive. Don't forget you already have these skills but have learned not to use them or not to trust them. Allow them to return, don't force them. Trying suggests failure. Allow these skills to resurface and develop gradually, in balance with your instinctive trust in those skills, so that your life flows peacefully from one mode into another. You may well feel different, and people may notice differences in you. Be prepared for a little scepticism from people you have been close to. This is their fear of change and it will influence you if you allow it to.

## *Internally referencing experiences*

Intuition is about becoming more self-reliant and internally referenced. By keeping this work personal and private, and doing it alone or with a trusted friend, you are already becoming internally referenced and independent of the opinions and advice of other people. Once you really trust your intuition you will become quite independent of others. This can be hard for other people who see your dependence as a security for themselves and their relationship with you. Being dependent on a best friend for making decisions and sorting out problems is a dependency relationship and this reduced need to confer can be threatening to friends. Allow your intuition to develop as a private experience and share it only with people after it is comfortable for you. Their insecurity will be less aroused if they can see the changes that have taken place and that the friendship is still intact.

Fighting or forcing intuition and self-development will make it more difficult, often taking longer and being more painful. But pretending you are not intuitive is a form of denial. All unhappiness is based on the fear which comes from not trusting yourself and being dependent on other people. This is a process of change. Taking things gently allows the changes time to take maximum effect, with minimum disruption or stress.

## Summary

Developing intuition is simply reclaiming your own birthright and heritage.

- ◆ We all have intuitive skills which can manifest in many ways.

- Many people have been trained to dismiss intuitive experiences and are no longer able to trust their own judgement.
- Developing intuitive skills allows you to live more closely to yourself and your own reality.
- Reclaiming your inherent skills is a gradual process and should not be rushed.

## Exercises

### Exercise 1

Spend a few moments, up to 30 minutes if possible, noticing everything around you. See how much information you pick up in the immediate present. Do this regularly, daily if possible. This is based on a Buddhist technique called mindfulness. It is an excellent way to become more aware of what is happening around you now, to be open to all the information you are often missing.

### Exercise 2

We have to know what makes us unsettled too. This is an ongoing exercise, over at least a week. Pick one day in a regular week of your life, not a holiday or special week. On that day record in your book everything that bothers or annoys you, or causes you to feel irritated or unsettled. Almost all stress relates to our resistance to changes, whether to routines, unexpected events, requests and demands, or other people's behaviours and attitudes. Use these headings:
- What was the event?
- Who was involved?
- What were your physical responses, e.g. stomach tightening, neck pain, clenched fists or jaw, headache?
- What were your verbal responses, e.g. speaking snappily, expressing anger or shouting, or withdrawing?
- How did this experience leave you feeling?

As you write down these experiences, you may find that your responses are changing in intensity, length, severity, etc. Record this too. Do this for one day, and forget about it for a week.

**Assessing yourself**

After one week take a look at what you wrote in the exercise above.

◆ Think through those experiences and decide if they still make you feel the same way.

◆ If your feelings have changed, how? What do you feel now?

◆ If your perspective has changed, how? What is your perspective now?

◆ What would you do differently if the same experience were to occur now?

◆ What is the positive outcome from this recorded experience?

◆ What have you learned about yourself from doing this exercise?

You might have learned a little more about yourself and how you respond to life. You may have started to recognise that you can choose how to behave rather than react, that you can take more responsibility for everything that you say, do, think or feel. Perhaps you found that things change over time. Could you now change your immediate perception and deal with things as if they were already a week old? It might be interesting to experiment with this; it is a choice you can make.

## Exercise 3

In your exercise book, record any dreams you have and date them. This can include dreams which you had some time ago and which left an impression on you. It can also include daydreams. Don't be tempted to look up meanings in dream dictionaries. These can be helpful but in the main it is better if you learn how to interpret your own personal, unique, mental imagery. The books tell you what to think. For this exercise it is more helpful to wait and develop your own ways of interpreting your experiences. Some ways of doing this are:

◆ Consider the images which have been presented to you -- how do they make you feel?

◆ Do they parallel aspects or influences in your own life experiences?

◆ Do meanings seem to develop after a period of time and reflection? If so, record these with the dates. Recording is more important at this point, rather than interpretations.

Keep a detailed account of any dreams you have and ask your subconscious mind, before you go to sleep, to send dreams which will guide you and allow you to remember them. Firmly intend to dream and don't worry if it doesn't happen immediately.

## Exercise 4

Think about what changes you can make in your routines, your family, work and time management, which will enhance your own natural rhythms and allow you to accomplish what you want to achieve. Make notes in your diary or workbook of all the rhythm changes you experience, and of your differing emotional states and how they relate to your own cycles.

## Exercise 5

If you want to access both sides of the brain at will, rather than waiting for the diurnal rhythm to reach its nadir, you can access your right brain with these breathing exercises.

1   Allow at least five minutes to settle and relax. Begin by placing a finger at the side of one nostril and pressing gently to close it. Breathe in, then quickly change fingers to close the first nostril and breathe out through the other. Then breathe in from the same side and change back to the first side to breathe out. By breaking each complete breath cycle into two halves, and alternating the inhalation and exhalation side, you access each side of the brain and get them working in harmony.

2   To completely access the right brain, lie on your right side for 5-10 minutes and you will find that your left nostril becomes clearer and then becomes the dominant breathing one. You can of course just hold your right nostril closed for a prolonged period of time and this will also access the right brain through the left nostril.

3   Sleeping on your right side can induce more intuitive breathing cycles and encourage intuitive dreams.

## Exercise 6

Find a quiet place to sit uninterrupted for some time. Make yourself comfortable and just see what happens. Let the thoughts float free-style through your mind, let the sounds around you register and drift away again. Don't worry if at first you find your thoughts seem to get caught on a runaway thought train; focusing on them will block your deeper intuitive knowing. Allow them to pass by, notice them, do not attach to them.

## Developing skills

Remember that practice makes perfect. This is easier said than done if you have been taught not to tune in to your intuitive skills Following chapters in this book will help you to unfold further skills. Just keep with it for now and wait for results to start to arrive in their own time. You can develop intuition, you can trust it, but you can never force it.

Tools reflect the
psychic or
emotional
energies
generated by the
seeker.

CHAPTER 4

# Choosing Your Approach with Tools

There are many ways of experimenting and learning. If you are uncertain about tools such as tarot, crystals or *I Ching* then this might also be a good time to explore the basis for your reservations as part of your belief system. Tools allow you to explore your intuition and psychic ability gradually as you build up your own confidence in this way of living. Try using one of these on a regular basis, keeping a record of your readings as part of your psychic or intuitive development and recognising your own internal symbolism. This will help you to interpret dreams later on. You can experiment with all three according to your mood.

## Valuing tools

Even for experienced psychics, tools simply give a focus for interpretation, providing more information about the issues being explored. They work by reflecting the energies being generated by the seeker. These are the psychic or emotional energies which we release (see Chapter 10). For now, try accepting that these energies exist, from the examples below, and recognise that we are all sensitive to them but mostly unaware of them.

You recognise energies when:

◆ You can sense what kind of mood someone is in before they speak.

◆ Some people make you feel differently after you have been speaking to them from before the encounter.

◆ You feel uncomfortable when some people get within a certain distance from you.

◆ You can tell if people have been previously arguing in a

room just before you enter, even if they appear to be smiling comfortably.

## *Reading energies*

All these experiences are readings of people's energies and we all do it. Emotions and thoughts all create an energy which is released into the atmosphere or universe. We know this and are all aware of it, but most of us can only sense the very strong energies, as when you walk into a room and two people have been arguing. They may deny it or attempt to conceal the truth, but if you sense the anger then know that you are right and allow your intuition to lead you. The cover-ups are attempts to deceive and teach us to mistrust our intuition. Parents especially should be wary of doing this to their children because you are deceiving your child and teaching them not to trust themselves. You may think that you are protecting them but no one needs protecting from anything that is true.

## *Using tools*

If you can relate to the concept of energy, you can accept that this is the basis of using tools. They reflect what is in your conscious or subconscious mind at the time of the reading.

> Different energies have different vibrations and will affect the tools in different ways, giving the variety of readings possible.

The tools explored here are very useful in getting specific answers to questions. They respond to energy vibrations from the subconscious mind of the person for whom the reading is done.

## Preparing to work with tools

Several points need consideration when working with tools. You should make it a habit to practise these each time you begin to work:

♦ Most tools are used with the left hand and therefore respond to the vibrations of the right brain – this is the part of the brain which governs intuition and the whole picture.

♦ Before working with any tool, spend a few moments reflecting on what you wish to explore.

♦ Allow yourself to relax deeply, to release all thoughts and feelings which may block the deeper, more subtle energies you want to work with.

♦ Allow thoughts and feelings to drift past you, notice them and let them go on their way.

♦ Even if you have a difficult situation for which you wish to consult the cards or *I Ching*, clear your mind as much as possible while you seek answers.

♦ Respect your tools and keep them carefully, making sure that they do not lie around collecting all sorts of other energies.

♦ Don't let others handle or use your tools, they are more effective when they work and respond to only your vibrations.

## Exploring the *I Ching*

The *I Ching* is based on the law of chance: the idea that nothing is accidental and everything has a cause and effect. It is also careful about accepting the idea of change. It is clearly established throughout the *I Ching* writings that changes in life will occur and we have choices of how to deal with them:

1   We can fight it.
2   We can flow with it.

The first option is a path of turmoil, pain and struggle and the second is a path of contentment. Which way do you think is the easiest way to live?

### Establishing the historical basis

The *I Ching* is a system of divining that has been around for at least 5,000 years and originated in China. Initially it was passed down orally through verses formatted by the sage Fu Sui in 600 BC.

Confucius wrote a number of additional commentaries and

called the whole body of work *I Ching*. It has continued to evolve as a philosophy for daily living, making decisions and seeking guidance.

## Establishing concepts of balance and influence

Taoism introduced the concept of yin and yang as the opposing life forces of male and female, suggesting these two energy forces are flowing into and away from each other constantly, thus establishing the concept of continual change. *I Ching* also means the Book of Changes. Confucius met Lao Tze, the founder of Taoism, in 517 BC, learning a great deal, but with the turbulence of Chinese history it was many years before Confucius was given an influential position in Chinese society. His position as magistrate was so effective in changing people's behaviour that he became minister for crime and collected many enemies who feared him. Ultimately he was removed from power as a result of jealousy and died convinced of his own failure to bring about permanent change. However, once news of his death spread, the wisdom in his teaching began to take force with an energy that could not have occurred if he had still been living, and his loss to Chinese society was recognised. Almost all Confucius' work was destroyed by later warring factions, except the *I Ching* and all his work and commentaries on them. Like all truly spiritually based methods of divining, the *I Ching* carries a strong moral and ethical code which is reflected in the summaries and can be applied to all levels of society, to the self and aspects of personal life.

## Underlying philosophy

The principle of *I Ching* is based on the opposing forces of male and female, yin and yang. These forces represent constant change and motion. The life goal of an individual is to remain true to themself and to live life welcoming and rising to the challenges of change. Change happens anyway but it is how we deal with it that counts. The *I Ching* reflects ideas to help us face changes, maintaining our self-respect and dignity without giving in to fear of the unknown.

Because western society has taught us to use the logical side of our brain, this increases our resistance to change enormously. It is this resistance which causes the pain and fear. one person's disaster is another's opportunity, but the perception is based on either fear or going with the flow. The *I Ching* represents going with the flow and dealing with what comes up. The intellect resists change if it does not seem like a choice. It prefers to give the impression that we can always control our choices. We *cannot* choose all that will occur in our lives. We *can* control our own behaviour, but this should be approached with a balanced and open mind. We should look for the learning from the situation, rather than reacting from fear-based reluctance to accept change because of its illusion of security. This attitude, or philosophy, underlies many, many aspects of intuitive work.

## Using the coins

*I Ching* works on the principle of throwing three coins, each with a head or tail side to it.

◆ each head side is worth 3 points
◆ each tail side is worth 2 points.

Thus you can have a score of between 6 and 9 for each throw.

◆ Odd number (7 and 9) throws are represented by an unbroken line
◆ and even numbers are broken lines (6 and 8).

The throws come in two sets of three and each set of three is called a trigram. So a reading would consist of the combined influences of two trigrams placed one above each other as they were thrown. Make a note of the value of each line so that you can look up a line of change, which is either a 6 or a 9 in certain positions.

**Case study**

The question: Will this book be a success and of benefit to many people? When thrown the coins came up with the following numbers: 9, 7, 6 and 8, 8, 8. Drawn they look like this:

In the Book of Changes this is Kuan which translates as View – Trigram number 20. The top trigram is a gentle wind, while the lower is the receptive earth. The image here is of the wind blowing the dust of the earth hither and thither, to no great effect. Looking at the hexagram as a whole, you can see that its appearance is similar to a tower. Towers were distinctive features of Chinese life and they symbolise being able to see out over the land and also being seen. The essence of this hexagram therefore has much to do with contemplation. It is a time likened to autumn, when you can take stock of your situation. Take this chance to examine your own values and make any changes you think necessary in the light of new experience. If you do this you will find that people will listen to you with a new appreciation. Your influence will grow more through this inward process than it ever could though any external actions.

The line of change is 9 at the top which reads:

*If you find yourself becoming rather remote from the situation be sure that this is due to your becoming genuinely 'moved on' rather than to your merely posturing.*

The line of change 6 in third place reads:

*Paying too much attention to your inner workings can be self-defeating. It is much more valid and telling to observe the impression you are making on the outside world.*

### Interpretation

'This is an opportunity for me to say some very important things which will influence many people, but I must be careful not to become like the dust blown in the wind and waste the opportunity. I must spend time and contemplate how I can best write this book. I also see the changes as telling me not to get carried away with success, ego-based motivations, but be true to myself and my belief that we all benefit each other in many different ways. If I allow my ego related to success to take over then I will damage myself and my work will be less significant, but if I write this book with care and love then it will benefit myself and all who read it.'_____

Most *I Ching* sets will give you more detailed instructions on how to use them, and will include the interpretations and lines of change for you to read. It is impossible here to include all the interpretations even briefly, since there are 64 trigrams and several possible lines of change with each trigram. If *I Ching* appeals to you then find a set you like and have fun.

## Exploring tarot cards

Tarot works in a similar way to *I Ching* using vibrations from the intuitive brain to guide the choice of cards. Again it is a tool to help you contemplate the influences around you, including past, present and future. You can choose from many different layouts as you become more familiar with tarot cards and their meanings. Remember to prepare in the same way as suggested above.

### Establishing the historical basis

Conflicting stories of how old Tarot is include claims that it originates from ancient Egypt and that even the word tarot comes from the name of the Egyptian god of magic, Thoth. It is also claimed that they were originally used by the Knights Templar around 1188. The earliest playing cards seem to originate in China and Korea in the 11th century. There are card decks dating back to 14th century Italy, which were used both for playing card games and fortune-telling. However, there are teachings that the images on tarot cards have much deeper meanings than a superficial game would suggest. The symbolism of some suits contains references to much deeper and older symbols of mysticism, with references to the teachings of the Gnostics, the Jewish Kabbalah and the orders of the Knights Templar and Rosicrucians. The illustrations of the Devil and High Priestess cards include a number of references to symbolism from long ago, much of it deeply metaphysical. (See Figures 2 and 3.)

### Establishing concepts of choice and destiny

It is largely accepted by tarot users nowadays that the reason tarot works is to do with the Jungian concept of synchronicity. Jung did a lot of research with the tarot, *I Ching* and astrology symbols and decided that coincidences in life had clearly

1  A cup of lambs' blood as used by the Greek priestesses at the temple of Apollo. If they obeyed the rule of chastity they would drink the blood and be granted the gift of prophesy.

2  Lamb on the back of her chair also symbolises purity and truth.

3  Casket and key – holds secret which only she has access to because she wears the key around her neck – representing wisdom open only to her because of her qualities.

4  Lizard represents the soul. An African tribe, the Santals, believe the soul leaves the body as a lizard, and touching the dried skin of a snake or lizard will protect from illness.

5  Books represent her wisdom, learning and continual search for understanding.

6  Candles represent enlightenment, also cleansing with smoke, sending prayers upwards.

7  Pattern on bodice of her dress represents her questing approach.

8  Sphere showing astrological symbols and signs, to be explored for insight and intuition.

9  She sits with her back to the darkness – symbolises her refusal to live in fear.

The High Priestess represents intuitive awareness, the virgin archetype, a daughter or spiritual woman, love without sexual desire. She seeks knowledge and represents patient study and learning, spiritual enlightenment, psychological insight and wisdom. She is a master of the occult and uses its power in a benign, spiritual way. She also represents the power of silence and meditation.

Fig. 2. Imagery and metaphor for the High Priestess tarot card.

1   Donkey ears represent a refusal to hear truth.
2   Repulsive physical body represents the absence of awareness of beauty.
3   Wings of bat symbolise flight in darkness, seeing the negative and avoiding enlightenment.
4   Horns, slightly curved, symbolise a weak spine, bowing to ignorance.
5   Animal legs indicate animal instincts being indulged without honouring them.
6   Pentacles inverted symbolise refusal to see truth, to be stubborn and out of harmony with yourself.
7   Hand raised above man and woman symbolises acceptance of the Devil's message that the material world is the only reality.
8   Man and woman, bound by chains of ignorance, become like the Devil.
9   The block is only half a cube and represents misrepresented truth.
10  Flaming torch represents false light, burning passion and desire for material world.
11  Navel indicates a human birth, i.e. the Devil is entirely a human concept.
12  Darkness is where the Devil comes from, he is part of it.

The Devil represents self-imposed limitation and difficulties, the power of negative thinking and fear. Often it is about not letting something go from your life, refusing to listen to your inner voices. It represents inhibitions and self doubts, feeling stuck and trapped, deceit, obsessions with money or power, greed and sexual gratification without love. The Devil tells us to look beyond our immediate fears and see the truth.

Fig. 3. Imagery and metaphor for the Devil tarot card.

defined patterns or purposes which may not be clear at first but can be seen if we choose to look for them. This seems to follow the idea that there is a divine plan to the universe and that the laws which govern the universe also govern our lives. We are part of the universe and therefore subject to the same laws – that all experiences lead to harmony or balance in life although the process of change may be turbulent if we resist it. This also reflects the ideas of Leibniz, of pre-established harmony and a divine plan, and ancient Greek views of the universal laws affecting everthing.

> I cannot believe that God would choose to play dice with the universe.
>
> (Albert Einstein)

Jung also acknowledged that the images of the cards, especially those of the major arcana, contain deep messages which speak to our unconscious minds. So tarot works by speaking to what we know deep within our unconscious minds, drawing out images which relate to the synchronicity of our life.

### Understanding the structure of a tarot pack

Tarot cards are the historical basis for the playing cards with which we are familiar, but contain additional cards. There are four suits and each pertains to one of the modern suits:

◆ **Swords** – Spades. Air – Gemini, Libra and Aquarius sun signs. Refers to mental issues and conflict, difficulties and challenges, opportunities for changes in career and business matters. Activity, accomplishment for good or bad, strength or force. Dislike of emotions and emotional experiences, logic and reasoning in linear form, head over heart, truth-seeking, insensitive to feelings, arguments and broken relationships.

◆ **Pentacles** – Diamonds. Earth – Taurus, Virgo and Capricorn sun signs. Refers to money, security of a material nature, reliability and plodding persistence, educational and study matters, selfishness, concerns with land and inheritance, thoroughness and pragmatism.

◆ **Wands** – Clubs. Fire – Aries, Leo and Sagittarius sun signs. Refers to choices, decisions, energy, travel, movement, growth and inner change. Modest people who achieve a great deal quietly. They also represent leadership, creativity and ambition.

♦ **Cups** – Hearts. Water – Cancer, Scorpio and Pisces. Refers to emotional matters, pleasure, happiness, love, family relationships, passion and deep feelings, emotional intensity, comfort, children. Friendly, caring workers. Moody, romantic and intuitive, tearful and sentimental, weak and unreliable, creative and dreamy, fantasy and illusions, concerned with the needs of others.

Each of the royals represents a character or stage of development/maturity:

♦ **King** and **Queen** represent adult male and female
♦ **Knight** represents young man
♦ **Page** represents child of either gender and young woman.

In each suit there are the usual ace to ten, plus four court cards King, Queen, Knight (Jack) and Page. In addition there are 22 cards called the major arcana. These represent specific qualities such as strength, temperance, justice, but also represent archetypes of humanity such as the High Priestess, the Hermit, the Fool, Death etc. They are numbered 0–21 and represent the spiritual path or growth from the Fool at 0 to The World at 21. The Fool represents open-spirited naivete, the beginning of the journey or a leap into the unknown. The World represents the culmination of all the cards, fulfilment, harmony, achievement of the ultimate goal. In many ways the Major Arcana cards represent a journey through life to new levels of enlightenment and self-awareness. Thus the Fool is the beginning of the voyage and the world is the conclusion. Perhaps the Fool is a card which reflects your place on your journey of self-discovery through this book.

There are no 'bad' cards but some are not so easy to live with. The 'worst' cards in the pack are the 8, 9, 10 swords. They represent the hardest difficulties, perhaps total failure on one level, but even this can be seen positively.

## Reflecting and learning

You can use the cards for meditation as well as for readings. Each one of these cards represents an aspect of humanity which you can choose to reflect on.

◆ **Death**. One day you might choose Death to meditate on. Think of all the endings in your life, of all the little deaths, and notice how each one may have seemed hard at the time but has cleared the way and made room for new growth in your life. Use it to change. It can be a joyous card which represents new challenge and learning. It also means that something will have to be lost, but the gain is always greater than the loss. It does not represent easy times but it is not a 'bad card' as is often believed.

◆ **High Priestess**. Another day you might choose the High Priestess and reflect on your spiritual development and progress, where you still have work to do and where you have made progress. This is the card of secrets and intuition, inner guidance and non-sexual love. It tells you to look into yourself to find the answers to questions of where to go next and how to do it most wisely. It is also about early memories and mental conditioning that you still have to release yourself from. If you turn over two cards together and get these two as a pair for the day, then it could be telling you that there is a need for change and to release something that you need to recognise. You could then turn a third card to see the area that needs to be challenged from within.

◆ **The Devil**. A difficult card to reflect on. It represents all the dark corners of our mind, all the jealousy, fear and anger that lies hidden but causing disturbance in life. You can use this card to reflect on your responsibility to work with and heal all these negative emotions. It also holds deeper mystical meanings. (See Figure 3.)

### Introducing simple layouts

Figures 4 and 5 show two layouts for regular use.

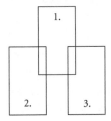

Fig. 4. Daily tarot card layout.

For the **daily layout** shuffle the cards well and meditate. Then spread the cards out in a long, overlapping sweep. Using your left hand, scan the cards for a few moments until one seems to pull you. Repeat this for the next two cards.

Card 1 is the main influence for the day, cards 2 and 3 allow you to see how this might manifest itself. There is no past or future beyond that day. It is a good reading to use for regular daily progress, allowing you to become familiar with what each card means.

## The Celtic cross layout

This is more suitable for asking for future influences and making decisions. You can use it to just see what it says or to ask a specific question.

**Case study: James plays with tarot**_____

James was playing with the cards and looking for some answers. There were all sorts of changes and redundancies at work which were making him feel very uncertain He was looking for reassurance and drew a Celtic cross spread. The 'final outcome' had the 10 swords. This felt bad. But there were other positive cards around him, for instance the 'environment' card was Ace of Wands which means new growth and learning, and the 'inner feelings' was 4 of swords which represents need for a rest, a chance to renew. This outcome was for his well-being but not what James wanted. Having accepted the insights that the cards gave him, when he had to compete and reapply for his own job and lost, it did not feel such a loss. The 'goal' card was the Wheel of Fortune which represents improvements and rapid change. With a reading like this it is easier to understand where your life is going and to look beyond the immediate, to see the bigger picture, which is intuition at work._____

**Case study: Asking questions from the cards**_____

The same question as for the *I Ching*, Will the book be a success?, was posed using the Celtic Cross layout.

- ◆ Card 1 reflects the questioner, me. In this position I drew the 2 of cups. This card means new romance and new beginnings, friendship, love union.
- ◆ Card 2 reflects the things crossing me, influences and obstacles, I drew the Queen of pentacles. This card means prosperity and well being, but this is an obstacle card so it might mean that I will have difficulties in this area whilst

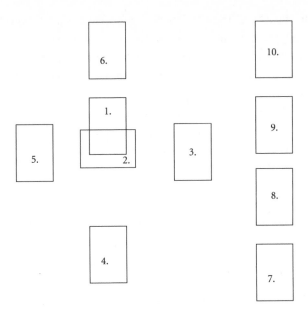

Fig. 5. Celtic cross tarot card layout.

writing the book, especially financial difficulties. Writing does not earn anything until it is complete and it still may not make anything, but in the meantime it takes a lot of time and I still have bills to pay.

◆ Card 3 is the card of distant past influences, and this card is the Knight of swords who represents progress and bravery, the unknown headlong dash into war. Writing this book is not a war in itself, but is based on a journey to rejoin myself and all the conflict which that incurs, so is a very relevant card.

◆ Card 4 is the recent past influences, and is the 10 of cups. This is one of my favourite cards as it represents great love, material comfort and spiritual peace. This is indeed a point I have reached in my life which has enabled me to write this book.

◆ Card 5 is future influences. It is the 2 of swords and this means being closed off to others, defensive, balance and harmony, offsetting factors. I read this to mean that the difficulties I face in writing this book will be balanced by the learning I gain. It will also require a lot of time to be spent alone writing.

◆ Card 6, the goal or destiny, is Justice, one of the major arcana. This is the final outcome and also represents harmony and balance, wrongs being righted and a fair outcome, good intentions. I feel this card reflects the previous five well and clearly suggests a very positive outcome.

◆ Card 7 is more about the questioner. The 10 of pentacles was drawn here and this is all the material security you could want. This brings me back to the question of financial reflections of the book. I think this will be met both during the writing and from publication.

◆ Card 8, environmental factors, came up as the Sun. This is also a major arcana card and one of my favourites. It means that everything favourable surrounds me.

◆ Card 9, inner emotions, drew as the 8 of pentacles. This card shows development, effort and learning, skill in business. I feel that this card reflects my own enthusiasm for writing this book and that it will achieve all that I hope for.

◆ Card 10 is the final outcome and I drew Jupiter, also known as the pope or hierophant. This card reflects intuition, divine guidance and inspiration. Since the book is about intuition and learning to trust the inner self, what better card could I have for the final outcome?

If I had tried to manipulate these cards to fall like this I could not have chosen a better combination of cards in their relevant positions. It is pointless to try to manipulate the cards since it will defeat the objective of laying them out in the first place.

## Reversing the cards

Every time you shuffle the cards you can choose to keep them all the same way up or shuffle them around each other on the floor or a table. This results in some of the cards being reversed or upside down. This brings a completely different meaning and an ever wider range of interpretations. Roughly speaking a reversed card means opposites:

◆ 10 of cups: upright – harmony in personal relationships; reversed – disrupted happiness

◆ 7 of pentacles: upright – slow and steady growth; reversed – giving up too soon.

## Answering questions

The cards are excellent for answering yes/no questions or looking at specific issues. Use them to support a more general feeling about something or someone, but never rely on them wholly for making decisions. They are *part* of a tool kit. Pull a card and then two more to support the first one and consider how they will influence you during the day. If you pull a card of difficulty, like the 8, 9 or 10 of swords, or the chariot or the tower, see this as an opportunity to learn something which might be hard but will be good in the end. Do not see the cards as foretelling doom and gloom, they are not intended to. They reflect your own vibrations and can be a good warning to change your attitude before it hits you from behind.

## *Choosing your pack*

Spend time deciding which images appeal to you most. There are many packs available, including mail order but, if you can, choose in person. The images have to speak to you as well as offering the accepted meanings.

## Exploring crystals

Crystals are slightly different from the two above because they are naturally formed substances and therefore have their own vibrations, according to the density of their molecules. For this reason they can be stronger to use and have a wider range of applications. Uses for crystals include:

◆ healing specific parts of the body
◆ psychic development
◆ divination of future and past
◆ meditating
◆ cleansing and balancing the chakras
◆ supporting intuitive insights through dowsing.

Dowsing is one of the more effective methods for working with crystals for developing intuition.

## *Choosing your crystal*

There are several methods of choosing crystals.

1   Go to a shop and hold each crystal for a few moments in your palm. When you find one which gives you a slight response, you have found your crystal. The response may come in the form of
    – a tingle
    – a light sense of warmth
    – a vibration in another part of your body, especially lower down near to the base chakra.

2    Wait until you are given a crystal which has been chosen for you by someone who loves you.

3    Choose a crystal which has the specific properties you require. For psychic development these are:

- quartz – attracts power and light and is an aid to opening the psychic centres and releasing higher consciousness
- rose quartz – unconditional love, a healing stone, used for relieving headache and migraines, both related to the brow chakra and therefore able to assist in developing spiritual and mystical abilities
- amethyst – known as the spiritual stone, it is said to help those who wish to develop psychically and protects from psychic attack. Sleeping with amethyst under the pillow is said to encourage intuitive dreams and inspiration
- amazonite – is useful for dealing with emotional difficulties and is good for preparation to begin this developmental work on yourself
- azurite – recommended by Edgar Cayce to aid psychic insight, also has good healing properties
- emerald – good for improving memory and intellect, and helps to overcome depression.

## Cleansing your crystal

As soon as you have got your crystal, cleanse it of any negative energy it may have collected. There are several ways of doing this:

- hold it in your hand under *cold* running water, a natural stream is best but a tap will do
- soak it in salt water for 24 hours
- stand it under a pyramid for at least 24 hours
- pray for it to be cleansed and sit in a circle of people all sending it the energy of love and healing
- visualise the crystal filling with white light and dispelling all negative energy, pass white light over it with your hand and convert all negative energy into positive energy and love.

## Using the crystal

Once you have cleansed your crystal, it's ready to use. If you wish to use it for answering questions, work with it on non-essential issues until you are used to its vibrations. Wearing it around your neck for 24 hours, permanently if you can, will connect its energy vibrations to yours. Then hold it in one hand and go into a deep, meditative state of breathing and sensing. Spend some time becoming acquainted with your crystal. Meditating with it is one of the best ways of building up this connection.

## Answering questions

The crystal as a pendulum can be very good for simple yes/no questions and can be used for prolonged conversations. Negotiate with your crystal for a direction of movement that indicates yes or no answers.

You may decide north/south swings for yes and east/west swings for no. A favoured one is a circular motion to mean yes, and a straight back-and-forth to mean no. Neither is right or wrong; just get used to how your pendulum works for you by concentrating very hard and repeating the word 'yes' to ascertain how it will move for this response, then repeat for 'no'.

Next start with simple questions to which you already know the answer to ensure that you are working clearly with your pendulum. Never try to trick it or test it with bad faith; you are only trying to trick or test yourself. If you try to direct the swing of the pendulum you are kidding no one.

## Avoiding misuse of tools

Many people believe that tools such as tarot cards are harmful. This is a misconception; nothing is harmful unless it is done with an inappropriate, manipulative approach. Then the risk is to the person trying to use them in this way and ultimately will rebound on them. Although readings done like this for other people can cause upset to the person concerned, this will correct itself and enhance the learning process. We all need to protect ourselves from negative influences. It is a belief in the negative power of tools that creates the problems, not the tools themselves – thought creates reality.

## Summary

Intuition is a celebration of life, so playing with it and around it is central to the experience.

◆ Tools are useful for obtaining answers to questions or exploring an insight in more depth.

◆ Tools work more effectively with regular use.

◆ Choose one approach which most appeals and develop this to a high level of accuracy.

◆ Experiment with other approaches as you grow in confidence.

◆ Keeping your tools personal to you is essential for clarity.

◆ Remember to play with your cards, crystal or *I Ching* and treat them with joyful respect.

*Most people only achieve a hint of all that they are truly capable of.*

# Clearing the Way

T wo of the main reasons people are unable to use or even recognise their intuition are:

◆ they do not know intuition exists in any real sense, i.e. knowledge based on supposed experience

◆ whatever experiences they have had, they have been taught not to trust it, i.e. emotion based on social or personal beliefs and value systems.

There are two ways in which these block us from developing our self-awareness and intuition:

◆ emotionally

◆ intellectually.

Both of these are ego blocks. Emotions are addressed in this chapter and intellect in a later one.

## Meeting the ego

Ego comes from the Latin 'I am' and was used by Freud to denote the part of the personality to do with reality – the way things are. He saw the personality as a balance between the id, which is the basic instinct urge, the ego and the superego which is the voice of our conscience, also called the internalised parent or guilt. It is the balance between these three that denotes personality. Western society has given the ego too much control, through beliefs in materialism and scientific reality. Intuitive development necessitates putting the ego in its place and using it wisely. An over-developed ego causes the individual to live in a state more biased towards fear. An ego-free person lives with more love and trust in their lives.

However, as a human we cannot be free from our ego. As Jung put it, we would not exist, we would die. In Buddhist terms this is a metaphorical death since the death of the ego is the goal, to end all suffering and fear. We do not die as people, but we die to the control of the ego over our lives, therefore becoming liberated from fear and becoming our true selves. Ego uses intellect and emotion to control our behaviours.

> Ego blocks are based on the existence of fear, which is the opposite of trust. If we live without the ability to trust ourselves, we live with fear and that can only be stressful and undermining, rendering us unable to achieve what we are capable of.

Most people only achieve a hint of what they are truly capable of and will even deny that they would want more. It can appear easier to hide from their fear of themselves than to confront it and open up to their true potential. This is not to deny the value of contentment; there is a distinction between true contentment and compromising one's potential in favour of an easier life. The latter causes unhappiness which comes out in stress-related illness and physical/social malfunction. Thus fear and mistrust become self perpetuating and effort is required to move beyond them. Each person is different in how this manifests and how they might change.

## Understanding emotions

Emotions are our messengers of experience. They tell us:
◆ this is a good experience, or
◆ this is not to be repeated.

We often shoot the messenger, i.e. we suppress or deny the emotion rather than deal with its causes. An emotion is the response to an experience. It does not exist in isolation, only in the context of experience or perceived experience. Emotions carry with them their own energy, which affects our perception of life because the energy fills our aura and filters our experiences.

## Understanding emotional cause and effect

Difficult energies or emotions are there to teach us. Once you accept their purpose, you no longer need to fear or avoid them. We all have to manage difficult experiences but we also need to recognise that these experiences reflect our own inner conflicts and difficulties. The negative emotional energies are the outcome, they are not the cause. They will influence the cause through some deep-seated fear we hold on to. The purpose is to highlight it so that we can recognise it and choose to let it go. It's a bit chicken and egg. If we hold a fear we will influence our own experience and bring that fear into reality. Until we release the fear we will continue to experience it as part of our reality. As soon as we recognise and release the fear we will be free from that influence in our life.

## Being responsible

We have to take full responsibility for all that we are experiencing and feeling, and work to clear it or else it will come back again. To break this down into stages:

◆ we are reacting to the energies or experiences around us in a learned pattern of responses which becomes our definition of 'normal'

◆ this prevents us from examining exactly what form of fear is underneath our experiences

◆ to stop repeating patterns of similar experiences we must look for the causes of our fear

◆ having recognised causes from our beliefs, we need to acknowledge their teaching and let them go.

So it is actually about letting go of the causes by working on them. This means that the energies or experiences change – if they return they work in less challenging ways. We must learn the lessons and move on.

## Breaking the repetitive cycles

One of the laws of experience is that if you do not get the lesson the first time, it will come back to you again and again, getting more traumatic each time, until it cannot be ignored.

You may experience it as a major crisis, but if you look back you can see that there were lots of warnings which you ignored. And eventually most of us do learn. You get to the point that you know the only way to stop yourself going round the same loop is to work on why you keep attracting those situations to yourself. Once your consciousness shifts enough, the endless cycles of repetition stop and life improves. New challenges will be presented, daily; you just become more adept at recognising and dealing with them. In theory it's easy, the difficulty arises in our resistance to change. The ego doesn't like change, it likes reality to remain stable and consistent, then it will 'know what to do' These are perspectives and perceptions which give us all the reasons we need to avoid this work, while at the same time convincing us of their rightness.

### Case Study: Jane Works on Forgiveness

Jane reads books about self-help regularly, and noticed that most of them talked about forgiveness and letting things go. She had difficulties in most relationships around her but wanted to find love in some form. Mostly it came in abusive forms. She spent a lot of time looking back at all the very abusive experiences in her childhood and thinking 'They're not going to get away with it, if I forgive them for what they did to me as a child, beatings and emotional manipulations, then I am saying it is OK that they did that to me and it is not'. Finally a small argument with a friend occurred and she found herself using this 'forgiveness and letting it go' approach. She felt much better immediately and realised that the argument was nothing really, almost that it had never existed. Then she thought about her family again and thought 'No, this is different, this is much bigger'. But gradually over the next few days she found herself thinking 'They are the same, and I can forgive here too because I do not want it any more and I am letting go of all these injustices heaped on me so that I never have to live with them again'. Immediately Jane started to feel lighter. She met new people who were gentle and kind and not interested in abusive relationships. _____

## Feeling better about yourself

The truth is **we have to let it all go.** If we continue to feel angry about past experiences we are only hurting ourselves – not the perceived perpetrators. They have moved on and possibly forgotten about us. Our pain does not hurt them, it hurts us. The fact that we are experiencing anything as a difficulty means that we are having a deep fear revealed to us. It is a messenger, flagging up what you need to do next to feel better about yourself from now on.

## Experiencing emotions

Many people in western society are brought up in the idea that:

◆ emotions stop you getting on with life

◆ emotions are a sign of low intellect or poor self-control

◆ you really need the logical, scientific approach to life to be successful

◆ expressions of stormy emotions are seen as socially unacceptable.

### *Repressing emotions*

Emotions are very important messengers because they are telling us something about ourselves. The mistake is to use them as 'evidence' of how other people are 'making us' feel. Instead of repressing feelings we need to lay them out and take a good look at them. The amount of energy required to hold down an emotion is enormous and wasteful, and sometimes we stuff down good emotions as well as difficult ones. If we could use this energy productively, we would feel much less tired and achieve a greater sense of peace in life. If we didn't suppress any part of ourselves, we could start to find out who we really are.

### *Denying good emotions*

Good emotions get ignored too. We deny our *right* to be happy. When things come along that show us that we are loved and all our needs are met, we often deny them because we say, 'I can't possibly be loved'. We do this in all sorts of different ways:

◆ compliments we reject from people, either denying or dismissing them

◆ if someone is generous we say 'Oh no, you shouldn't have done that for me'

- if something good happens, immediately looking for the catch or flaw
- assuming the worst from every situation and person, especially rejection or betrayal
- assuming that whatever we have received will also be lost equally easily, or taken from us
- assuming that if we have this it cannot be worth having in the first place
- thinking that anyone who gives to us must be defective in some way.

Even if we accept the 'gift', we have negated the right to give and receive that generosity for both parties. The metamessage, or belief behind our responses, is:

- We do not deserve good things in our lives.
- We want them desperately but we cannot allow ourselves to have them.
- We fear that if we have good things we will lose them again, so it's better not to have them in the first place.
- We don't know how to accept this love or attention.
- We are frightened of being excellent, being different, standing out from the crowd.

So we attract styles of life and love which reflect that belief, we attract love that is not in our best interests because we do not believe we are entitled to love which is. All this occurs at a subconscious level, but you may have recognised at least one of your own inner voices above, or can think of similar ones telling you not to trust.

## Falling in love

When we fall in love with someone and feel happier than before because of it, we often believe that the other person is responsible for this. By so doing we are giving them the power to make us happy or unhappy. All happiness, however, comes from within. To believe differently is an illusion which denies our responsibility for our own feelings. So when we are loved we are looking at ourselves from a new perspective, one that has been revealed through the eyes of another.

A new lover shows us a new perspective of ourselves and perhaps our own greater capacity for happiness. They enable us to find new ways of looking at ourselves and discovering more of our true nature. This reveals to us new and deeper levels of our own intrinsic happiness to which we had previously been blind. This is known as *mirroring*. All that we like or dislike in others reflects all that we like or dislike in ourselves. That which we dislike reflects our ego defences, fears and self-justifications.

If in the name of love we seek to protect the other from these reflections, we are also denying them the right to know themselves and make their own growth and progress in self-discovery. If we protect we disempower using an illusory concept of love as a justification. Love needs feedback which is honest, and free from guilt or fear, if it is to grow healthily. Self-love is the first step in achieving the loving relationship we want with others.

## Recognising negative self-concepts

One of the best ways of assessing how good you feel about yourself is to monitor your thoughts and opinions about other people. If we don't have a good opinion about ourselves, it is impossible to hold good opinions of others. If we feel good about ourselves, we do not need to have critical or judgemental attitudes about other people. If you were comfortable with it in yourself, you would not react to it in others. A criticism of someone else is really a criticism of yourself, and a judgemental approach to life is a direct reflection of how you feel about yourself.

> To be happy we must not be too concerned with others.
> (Albert Camus)

## Understanding discernment

There is a fundamental difference between criticism, judgement and discernment.

- ◆ A *criticism* is a reflection of something you do not like in yourself that you have identified in someone else as a basis for assessing them into categories of right or wrong, good or bad.

- ◆ *A judgement* is a decision that something is right or wrong, and assumes that people intentionally do wrong instead of making mistakes and learning lessons.
- ◆ *A discernment* is an attitude of acceptance and choice, based on the idea that we are all doing the best we can with what we know, even if that is not very sensible. We might not choose to behave as we observe someone else doing but we do not condemn them for doing so, they have their lessons to learn and we have ours.

> There can be no real freedom without the freedom to fail.
> (Eric Hoffer)

What does it mean when we know that we are messing up and we still do it?

You may partially understand what it is you need to know, but until you have fully explored all the negative aspects it is not possible to fully understand the positive. So it is still part of your learning and therefore the best you know at that time.

Once we start to feel better about ourselves, and recognise our learning processes instead of judging and criticising ourselves, we no longer need to judge others. We are free to start accepting more love into our lives. As self-esteem increases we are able to accept good experiences into our lives.

## Suppressing negative emotions

What we really suppress are the negative emotions, because we don't want to:
- ◆ know that we are scared about so many things
- ◆ know that these things make us angry
- ◆ know that we did this wrong
- ◆ be responsible for sorting things out.

Therefore we blame other people. This comes back to criticism and judgemental attitudes to self and others, transferring our negative thoughts about ourselves onto other people. We have to start forgiving ourselves for being human and making mistakes, because there isn't a human alive who doesn't. If you keep doing what you've always done, you'll keep getting what you've always got. You have to change in order to get something different. And you're the only person who can change.

## Relating emotional balance to better health

Having made the change towards forgiving ourselves and other people, we can start looking at the emotions which are coming up. Here we may have some strange experiences. Physical manifestations may happen. People often get sore throats when they are not expressing themselves clearly. Suppressed emotions are things we need to get 'off our chest'. So suppressing emotions keeps them locked inside our physical bodies and undermines our immune system, leaving us susceptible to the micro-organisms which attack that part of our body. For instance streptococcus bacteria are in our throat most of the time so why do we not have a sore throat most of the time? (See Chapter 10.) All emotions are about us. When we think we're annoyed with other people we're really annoyed with ourselves for one or more of the following reasons:

◆ they have wrong-footed us and we allowed it
◆ we have not responded as we would have preferred          ·
◆ our weaknesses have been exposed
◆ our behaviour has been mirrored back to us
◆ we have not yet learned to accept that we are not perfect
◆ we fear the criticism and judgement from others for our imperfections.

Because all of this is unexpressed, either externally or internally, it gets stuck. The term 'we need to get it off our chest' is a clear indication of what we are truly doing. The blocked emotion becomes a physical reality, a blocked chest, throat, etc. Lower back pain can relate to early childhood, upper back pain more to current pressures and burdens – a yoke of responsibility on the shoulders.

The body is a physical manifestation of our emotional state. The more we release negative emotions the more we find our lives feeling healthy and full of vitality.

The mind-body overlap relates to the fact that the body is a completely self-supporting organism which is able to fend off hostile organisms very effectively if it is running on full capacity. If it is not, then something can break through our defences and make us ill. Thoughts create reality here too!

> I have never met a healthy person who worries very much about his health, or a really good person who worries about his soul.
>
> (J B S Haldane)

### Case Study: Jane Releases Fear

Jane found that she was a lot less ill with coughs, sore throats and colds once she started to clear away all the stored up negative emotions from her childhood. She also learned to say what she felt in the present and not be silenced for other people's comfort, to be true to herself. Jane also had problems with cold hands and feet in winter. This represented her fear to reach out in love in case she got rejected again.

## Connecting feelings and physiology

These parallels seen in the case study are not so difficult to follow. We withdraw and so our blood withdraws. The same with our feet, we have 'cold feet' i.e. reluctance to move forward, to change and develop and to try out a new situation. Much of our language reflects this body/mind overlap, yet we do not acknowledge the basis of real truth behind these sayings. Circulatory diseases such as clogged up arteries represent our clogged up emotions. Anger causes a stroke or heart disease. Diet, smoking and lack of exercise add to the risks involved, but they will not cause it if we are free-flowing in our bodies emotionally. This is why some people smoke all their lives and have no ill effects at all and some people eat completely the 'wrong diet' yet still maintain a very fit, healthy and long life.

## Distinguishing between responsibility and blame

To achieve excellent health from mind/body interaction alone requires personal growth and development. There has been a tendency in recent years to make people feel almost to blame for their own illness. It is unkind to imply someone's illness is caused through lack of emotional expression and is their fault. Remember:

◆ We are all doing the best we can with what we know.

◆ We can only release things at the level of understanding we have reached.

◆ For most people these ideas are still in the early stage of contemplation and exploration.

◆ Most people are not fully aware of themselves and are therefore unable to master their health either.

◆ While we live in a human body we are going to be susceptible to human experiences, which will include repression of emotions and illness.

If we also accept that our beliefs create our reality, while we believe in the existence of physical illness as a fact which we cannot control, then that will be the experience we have, fully and completely and without exception. This will increase the likelihood of our blocked emotions causing, manifesting and releasing themselves as illness.

People use illness for years, either consciously or unconsciously, to protect themselves and to get what they need, either a rest or some attention and care which they believe they would not otherwise get.

**Case Study: Simon Needs Rest**

Following the break-up of a long term relationship, Simon had been out almost every evening and weekend. He met someone he liked and they planned a whole weekend together. On the Friday evening he became ill with flu and was unable to do anything except sleep for the whole weekend and a few days into the next week. He had to rest and spend time alone.

Simon also often got bad headaches. When he explored them further he found it was bottled up anger and frustration. He now releases his frustration in other ways, e.g visualisations. He now experiences headaches less often and is able to release them soon after they start.

## Mind/body influences

Even though we can acknowledge our lesson, we still may have some difficulty in mastering and ending the pattern completely. The key to all this is to keep reminding yourself that you are doing the best you can with what you know. More examples of mind/body influences expressed through language are:

◆ a pain in the neck
◆ gets my back up
◆ cold feet
◆ get it off your chest
◆ a lump in the throat
◆ broken-hearted
◆ like a punch in the guts
◆ took my breath away
◆ millstone round my neck
◆ my hands are tied
◆ and then it hit me.

There are many examples of language expressing our emotional/physical states, without us being aware of what we are really saying. Perhaps you can think of some more.

## Learning from illness

Accept that the human body may succumb to illness and eventually you will achieve better health. Illness is also a teacher in our lives. Illness teaches us to:

◆ be a patient/victim – or not
◆ surrender to our need for help – interdependence
◆ trust that others will care for us
◆ not be in control – let go
◆ be passive, inactive and silent – contemplate or meditate.

Many people state that they are not good patients and hate to be ill. For many losing good health is the worst thing that they can imagine. This becomes a very real fear which can turn into a reality, a self-fulfilling prophesy. Hence the earlier quote.

Illness also teaches others around us to be tolerant, compassionate, patient, generous, forgiving. In turn, illness can teach us and bring to us similar qualities that we may not have had otherwise. So we will have illnesses which will be lessons in what we need to learn, experience and release, expressing themselves in different ways. We have a human body and it is vulnerable to illness and disease, while we believe that it is.

## Emotionally changing our body chemistry

Positive emotions remain free within us and allow the release of endorphins. Negative emotions are suppressed, causing further body changes, most notably suppression of the immune system. The damage is caused by the *suppression*, not by the emotion. So the first thing we need to do is to start noting exactly what our emotions are:

◆ Notice and acknowledge both positive and negative emotions in a mindful, observant way.

◆ Recognise that we can choose how to respond to other people's behaviour and treatment of us. It is our own attitude and response that hurts us.

## Controlling and accepting

Look at the next series of statements and decide which are true for you.

◆ I get cross when people do not behave as I think they should.

◆ I have absolutely no right to expect anybody to do what I want them to do.

◆ People find me 'difficult' because I do not behave in a way that suits them.

◆ I prefer to choose my own value systems and behaviours, rejecting those not in line with how I am as a person.

◆ Those who do not seek to control me do not find me difficult and when I do not seek to control others, I do not find them difficult at all.

◆ Every human being has an absolute right to think and feel as they choose and a right to make their own mistakes.

◆ The minute we make someone else responsible for our happiness we also make them responsible for our unhappiness.

Look at your responses to each of the statements above and answer the following questions in your diary.

1   Do you really want to be that much out of control of your own feelings?

2   Would you want that much responsibility for someone else's feelings? You could become a 'slave' to their happiness – is that all right with you?

## Happiness on condition

Happiness and contentment can only develop in one place – inside. Yet we have been conditioned to believe that it comes from something happening *to* us. Everything will be all right:

◆ if we get a husband/wife/partner
◆ if we get this job
◆ if we get that house
◆ if we get this salary
◆ if we get that holiday/car, etc.

## Turning everything into a positive

If we learn to accept that something makes us angry or unhappy, we can also choose to experience happiness because it has taught us something. We might feel unhappy for a while, but not in the victim sense. We can begin to welcome it and learn from the experience. Achieving this approach to life takes adjustment and there will be setbacks. But with perseverance it can become second nature. If you adopt this attitude you will begin to feel better. So if something makes you unhappy, turn it into a positive learning experience. Intuition is seeing the bigger picture, seeing it from all perspectives and not being a 'victim'.

## Accepting the messages

Emotions are our messengers not the *message*. If, for example, you recognise anger, ask yourself these questions.

◆ What does this tell me?
◆ What am I really afraid of?
◆ What is it not being recognised, how am I not getting what I think I need?

◆ Is it just the illusions which confuse me, through the value system of our society?

◆ Everything I need, I already am. Have I forgotten it and succumbed to the idea that my needs are met outside?

◆ Do I need to be angry or frightened?

◆ Right here, right now is there anything to be worried or frightened about?

If you arrive at the answer 'right here, right now there is nothing to be worried about', then don't be. If you do you are spoiling the very moment which could be lived in pure joy. Let the emotion go.

Remember, it was only a messenger not the message. If we do not acknowledge our emotions, we carry on in spite of them and ignore the opportunities to learn and let them go. Then we get the pains in our necks or backs, or our stomachs start churning and we transfer the emotion to our physical body. The body is saying 'You're not listening to me, I want to say something' and the subconscious mind says 'If you won't listen to me one way I'm going to find a different way to make you'. Then we start getting ill. It doesn't need to get that far.

## Practising forgiveness

Now you are ready for another challenge.

Every single experience you have ever had has been for your own benefit, however bad it was at the time.

> Adversity is the state in which a (man) most easily becomes acquainted with himself, being especially free from admirers.
>
> (Samuel Johnson)

This is a dramatic statement and you are probably thinking immediately of all the things that cannot possibly fall into that category. Allow your intuition to look more closely. Gradually you may understand that it is true, for many different reasons, some of which will become clearer as we work through the book.

Every experience you have ever had has taught you something. There is *positive* learning and *negative* learning. But all learning is to our advantage.

## Positive learning

Positive learning allows us to:
- Recognise our own responsibility in the event/outcome.
- See how not to behave.
- Recognise things in others that we do not choose to have in our lives and recognise their right to be however they are.
- Recognise what we have learned, i.e. what to do or not do next time.
- Have better coping skills in similar events.
- Look for warning signs and be better prepared.
- Learn things about ourselves that we did not know before.
- Heal ourselves and forgive ourselves for having got into that situation in the first place.
- Forgive others who are part of that and recognise that they also taught us valuable lessons.
- Move on and make our life even better than it was before.

## Negative learning

Negative learning allows us to:
- Retreat further into a protective shell.
- Blame other people for whatever has happened.
- Restrict our lives in order to protect ourselves.
- Treat all other people/circumstances with suspicion.
- Remain angry and bitter.
- Perpetuate the damage the original event caused by remaining a victim.
- Perpetuate the damage caused by the original event by repeating the action against others before they get you.

This teaches far more about victimhood and how life feels from this perspective. Whatever has happened to us in life, including all major forms of abuse, the sooner we can forgive ourselves and the abuser, the more quickly we can continue to live and enjoy our life.

## Understanding forgiveness

Forgiving someone is not for their benefit at all. It may help them to feel better about themselves and less likely to 'attack' again. It is only through healing ourselves that we forgive others, and by forgiving others we also forgive ourselves. Forgiveness is not saying that it is acceptable to have been abused or unkindly treated, it is saying that you do not allow the abuser to continue abusing you for the rest of your life.

## Hanging on to hurt

If we feel wronged and angry about something, the anger we feel hurts our own body, not that of the abuser. What is more it drives other people away because we release angry, negative energies and these are not pleasant to be around.

Consider these questions:

◆ Have you ever been near an angry person and felt their energy in their aura?

◆ How does it make you feel?

◆ Do you want to be near that person?

◆ Is that what you want to be like to be near?

Any retention of negative experience and emotions closes us down on ourselves. Living intuitively is a process of opening up to yourself and everything around in much finer detail. Releasing each and every experience you have ever had, looking at the experience and seeing it for what it really was – an opportunity to learn more about yourself than you could have learned in any other way at that time – allows you to become more open and clear-sighted about yourself and your reality. In many ways living intuitively is also living healthily, both emotionally and physically.

Forgiveness is a key to unblocking trapped emotions. It is a crucial step to allowing a free flow of energy right through our mental and physical experience. This is intuition working freely.

**Case Study: Susan Releases Anger**

Susan felt very angry with life. Her parents had been very critical of everything she had ever done, said or thought, so she had learned to keep quiet and not express herself. But inside she seethed and if friends said the wrong thing, or spoke about parents in general, she would release some of this angry energy and bitterness. She could not understand why people often liked her in the beginning but then backed off and found it hard to be close to her. She became more and more angry with life, feeling wrong, rejected and worthless. Yet her intuition told her she was really a lovely person. She couldn't understand why other people could not see what a lovely person she really was. One day a friend told her what a drag it was hearing about her parents and everyone was sick of it. The friend was fed up and told Susan to shut her up. Her parents were still hurting her even though she was now an adult. It made Susan realise what she was doing and she learned to begin to release the anger._____

## Summary

Knowing all aspects of ourselves means opening our eyes and releasing the debris we cling on to.

- ◆ If we are to open up our existing abilities and become reacquainted with what we already have, then we must release all emotional and intellectual blocks.
- ◆ Releasing our own negative emotions and seeing all experiences, however horrendous at the time, as positive learning, frees us and prevents the damage continuing.
- ◆ We can allow ourselves to work slowly in all aspects of this development, knowing that it is an unfolding of our true inner selves.
- ◆ There is plenty of scientific research evidence for intuition.
- ◆ Living in closer harmony with ourselves through listening and trusting ourselves can only bring about a better quality of life.
- ◆ Keeping an open mind to all aspects of our humanity, and especially of our potential, can only lead to greater achievement on both individual levels and as a society.

## Exercises

### *Exercise 1*

Spend one day monitoring all your critical thoughts and judgemental attitudes to both yourself and other people. Notice specifically what it is you feel critical about and make notes of similarities in your thoughts and judgements. Are your criticisms the same or slightly different from those of other people? Does this reflect the differences in how you feel about other people? How does this exercise make you feel about yourself? Now begin to reverse each critical thought you have. Look at the thought and see it from the perspective that we are all doing the best we can with what we know. How does this make you feel towards yourself and others?

## Exercise 2

Make a note of the terms you use and reflect on what they really are telling you. Think of your own possible mind/body overlap experiences. List any recurring health problems and physical difficulties

## Exercise 3

Become mindful. Stay consciously present. Start by picking a day and tune in to yourself regularly: 'Right now what am I feeling? What is my body saying?' Not being defensive, gently and uncritically allow yourself to be whatever you are and monitor it. Get to know yourself properly.

*Time is an important factor in all aspects of this work.*

# Experiencing Time Differently

M ost of the time people have psychic experiences and intuitions, hunches and gut feelings, but fail to notice them. This is usually due to the pace we live our lives at, and the way we relate to time itself. Time is an important factor in all aspects of this work.

♦ The more you *try* to achieve and rush through everything, the less you accomplish.

♦ The more you enjoy the doing in your own time, the more you achieve without noticing it.

As soon as you think about all the things you are supposed to do, you immediately sense the beginnings of panic in your stomach.

By being calm and relaxed we maintain our stamina. Being calm and relaxed also means being open to all those intuitive signals. If we do not allow ourselves time to notice the clues and hints we are given, we cannot truly work intuitively with our inner selves.

**Case Study: In the Garden**

'When I am sitting in the sunshine in my garden, letting time drift by, not worrying about anything, enjoying the sights and sounds around me, the insects around my pond and the birds who visit the trees, I consider myself to be working on my intuition. I am quietly noticing all that is happening to me, inside and out. I am taking time for myself to replenish my left brain resources and energies by allowing my right brain to lead me where it will. I do not limit this time unless I have a specific deadline, but I choose times when I will not need to break off early. I rarely continue for longer than an hour in this way, but if I do then it is nourishing the parts of my mind that serve me so well. The positive benefits of this are:

♦ Sometimes answers to questions appear for me.

♦ I can 'see' things in different ways and from different perspectives.

◆ My brain and mind feel rested and the next task is not a strain.

◆ I can work for far longer hours and not feel tired.

◆ Difficulties and challenges in life fall into long-term perspectives, making them easier to deal with.'_____

## Understanding time

Using intuition means getting a sense or an idea of what is to come in the future, making innovative connections with events from the past, and seeing patterns. It can be very strong and clear in its direction, or it can act as guidance for which options, from a number, you should take. Sometimes it can be just that change is imminent. So how can we possibly know what hasn't happened yet? In order to understand what you are working with it is essential to understand a little more about time as a medium of experience, rather than just **measurement**.

> The only reason for time is so that everything doesn't happen at once.
>
> (Albert Einstein)

## Conceptualising time

Since time is an abstract concept related to the measurement of existence, there is some need to put a form around it so that we, as humans, can relate to it. The common mistake is to believe these concepts represent all that time can be.

Time is rather like the universe itself. We cannot possibly know what it is but we can experience it in as many ways as possible, no limits.

### *Linear time*

past → present → future

This suggests that time passes in a straight line, from past to present to future. If this is the case the past can only be accessed through memories, and the future not at all because it hasn't happened yet so there are no energies released which your intuition can sense to tell you how to respond. There are two difficulties with this explanation:

◆ it is very reductionist in that it assumes this is all that time is: a line or chain of events

◆ it ignores many other experienced aspects of time which will be explored below.

The linear approach is a very left brain concept of time because it is empirical, we can measure it and plot it. There is also a contradiction here – the left brain, scientific assumption, that this is all there is to time, is rather missing the point because it is science which is attempting to go beyond all of this and explain the universe in terms of time being infinite and simultaneous. (See Chapters 8 and 12.)

## Cyclical time

This is a more flexible view of time, reflecting the idea that time has its seasons and follows the cycles of nature, of birth and death. Time is measured in the year, through seasons and through concepts of growth and decay, which are two sides of the same reality. We cannot have rebirth without making way for it, something has to go and the ground be prepared for new life, new experiences. This is the reality of death, a natural part of living, yet we fear it. Most of western society is afraid of death and no longer respects it as an essential part of life itself.

Letting go of that fear is one of the biggest emotional releases available to us all. The fear of endings/death is one of the most limiting beliefs we have. Clairvoyancy can tell of endings, including death, and we are afraid to embrace this as part of the essential cycles of living. In the tarot this is represented by Death, the Chariot, the Tower and other cards.

This concept also misses the point because it still accepts the idea of a progression through the spiral, or else an endless cycle which just repeats itself. Yet history can show us that although we repeat mistakes, they are never identical and if time were truly cyclical then it would repeat itself exactly. Each cycle is different from the next, so where does time begin and end?

## Time being measurable

This idea suggests that time is limited and, if it is to be measured, has a beginning and an end. Yet all the research to date on the origins of the universe are unable to even approach this question. Stephen Hawking brushes the question aside when asked where the seed of energy, which grew into the big bang, came from. The concept of infinity is hard for humans to take on, but infinity does mean with no beginning and no end, therefore immeasurable.

## Biological clock

Physically the biological clock is located in a group of cells called the suprachiasmatic nuclei. This is found in the hypothalamus and close to the optic nerve. It is strongly linked to and affects our circadian rhythms of night and day. Originally it responded to the rising and setting of the sun, but electricity has broken down these boundaries and we no longer experience darkness as a real part of our lives. In fact we try to eliminate it with street lighting, floodlighting etc. This both extends the 'working' day and desensitizes us to the subtle rhythms of the planet.

Close to the suprachiasmatic nuclei is the pineal gland, which is commonly accepted as the third eye and is linked to the brow chakra energies. The hypothalamus and pineal glands form part of the reptilian brain and are seemingly both linked to sight, foresight and light sensitivity. This suggests that time and sight are interconnected.

**Case Study: The Cave Experiment**_____

A cave explorer called Michel Siffre agreed to spend seven months living underground in a cave. He took with him all that he would need for the duration including food, books to read, artificial light and monitoring equipment. But *no* clock. His only link with the outside world was a telephone which was permanently manned in case of emergencies. He also had a computer and video link camera so that almost all his movements were monitored. Siffre established his own routine and went about his life, but it was noted that his biological clock went forward by about one hour per day. That is, he fell into a 25-hour routine day cycle. He went to bed an hour later each day, slept for the same length of time and rose one hour later._____

It is believed that the sun is a natural time-giver, and most of nature responds to its cycles and seasons, its heat and light energies which tell trees that it is spring, summer, autumn and winter, with all that each season brings. It is the natural controller of our biological clock too. It is important to notice the relationship between this section and the natural rhythms discussed in Chapter 3.

## Plato's theory

This is a more flexible approach and is still standing strong after all these centuries. He divided time into two concepts:

◆ One loosely follows both linear and cyclical explanations, which relates to the concept of imperfection, with seasons of birth and decay.

◆ The other relates to the concept of perfection and is infinite, from the god Chronos who created the egg from which the cosmos was born. He lives and exists in perfect time, everlasting and eternal, unmeasurable and extremely hard for human brains to grasp in any intellectual way.

If you can grasp a concept of time like this, you are probably working intuitively and feeling it rather than understanding it. Time is part of the cause-and-effect law of the universe. Past, present and future all affect each other through the connections of universal energy.

## Experiencing *déjà vu*

Déjà vu is a very strong experience when it does happen. Even for those who are familiar with it, it can be quite shocking and even frightening. So what is it?

You are walking down a street and you suddenly realise that you know where you are, what is happening and what is about to happen. You feel slightly queasy or excited inside and may be shocked by the clarity of the experience. It is certainly not subtle although it can leave you uncertain as to what is going on and how you can possibly know. It could make you doubt yourself.

If you fully understood the concepts of time above, and

recognise time as an experience rather than as a measurement, deja vu becomes quite easily explained as a time loop. The experiences are hints that there are glitches and loops in time, i.e. you have been here, done this, or seen this before, and you know what will come next. As you progress more and more with your intuitive development, these experiences will become part of the flow of life and stop seeming so extraordinary.

## Recognising synchronicity

This term was first used by Carl Jung to explain how coincidences just seem too significant to be explained away as chance. It is too intense and relates to a combination of several influences:

◆ thoughts

◆ dreams

◆ feelings

◆ events.

**Case Study: Margaret's Meeting**_____

Margaret was having all sorts of problems, reminding her a lot of a boyfriend she'd not seen for ten years. They had grown in different directions but some parts of their relationship had been very good. These were the areas of her life which were seemingly falling apart right now. She found herself thinking and talking about Pete quite often for a couple of weeks. She was surprised to be so preoccupied with thinking about him. Three weeks later she was with friends on a day trip to the coast. While walking along the promenade, who should be walking the other way but Pete. He had been thinking about her and tried to get in contact. He'd decided at the last minute to get on a train and come down for the day, quite unplanned._____

This is synchronicity, and it can threaten or challenge all that we believe in linear time and individual human understanding. It can feel very strange. Many people dismiss it as just coincidence, but if you look closely it is much more than that.

## *Explaining synchronicity*

One effective explanation is that we create these experiences ourselves, through the combined working of our conscious and unconscious minds. We are in a situation which the unconscious mind recognises and refers to previous experiences in a more creative way than we could logically think out for ourselves. Then it sends strong messages to the left brain which sets trains of thoughts in motion. Meanwhile the unconscious mind is still working on its own hypothesis and is showing this through day or night dreams. The combined energy of all this work will be sending very strong vibrations into the universe. This will be picked up by someone or something receptive to this vibration and respond to it accordingly. Margaret was sending out a message of help at both unconscious and conscious levels and Pete, who was still very fond of her, picked them up. This drew them to a point where they would be at the same time and the same place.

## Experiencing past, present and future

We all experience time in different ways and these differences will influence our interpretations and perceptions considerably.

We all place our individual emphasis on the past, present and future. The importance of experiences is related to where we keep our memories and there is a physical relationship with the body.

### Locating ourselves in time

Some people are so obsessed with events that occurred in the past that they still live there more than in the present. Others are so worried about the future that they cannot enjoy anything in the present. We all have some of each of these; it is the degree to which it affects us which is significant. As with everything else, there is no wrong or right but there is more or less comfortable.

> The key to intuition is living in the present and putting all of your awareness into this moment. By becoming very aware of the present we are able to pick up the cues and signals from around us and respond to them intuitively.

If we are too located in either the past or the future we will overlook these cues and create an uncertainty about the present which leads to all sorts of levels of fear and anxiety. Figure 6 shows different ways of experiencing time.

◆ **Example A.** This person has the past immediately above them and can feel it pressing down onto their head and shoulders all the time. The present is in front of them so they are disconnected from it, and the future is off at an angle to their right so they have to make a conscious effort to see it.

◆ **Example B.** This person has the past trailing immediately behind them and they are able to forget about things quite easily. However, the present seems to be happening all around them and they are not really connected with it either. The future is off at a wide angle, they can see this if they choose to look but it is somewhat obscured by the present whirring around them.

◆ **Example C.** This person has the past straight in front of them and they are quite detached from the present which is off to the side. The future is almost completely blocked from view by the past.

◆ **Example D.** This person has the present within their experience, they live completely within their present but can quite clearly see where it is leading to in the future. They are moving ahead in their life and will get where they are going with comfort and intuition. The past is nicely tucked away behind, but at an angle which makes it less likely to press down on them or catch them up. It can easily be seen and referenced for the valuable learning resource that it is.

## Recording your progress

As with any skill which you are developing, albeit one which you already have within you, you will spend some time practising and getting it right and also making mistakes. This, too, will take time. When a baby first learns to walk they do not see the first fall as evidence that they will never be able to walk, they just keep on practising until the new skill is mastered. Thus it is with intuition and spontaneous living. You are the toddler learning this new skill and making mistakes is an essential part of that learning process.

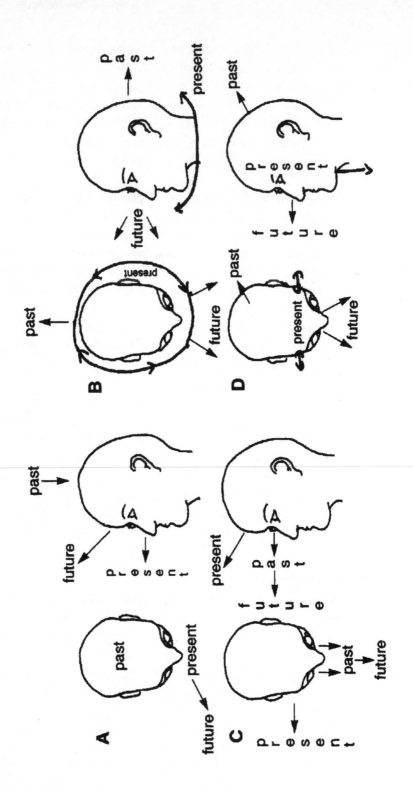

Fig. 6. Spatial experience of time (time lines).

> Character building begins in our infancy and continues
> until death.
>
> (Eleanor Roosevelt)

Without the mistakes to see when it is not working, you will
not be able to discern between true intuition and ego voices. It
is important to notice:

◆ how you make mistakes
◆ what the difference is between getting it wrong and getting
  it right.

Trial and error is one of the most valuable resources you have
in making sure that you develop your skill. Developing
intuition thoroughly and reliably is really a case of more haste,
less speed, but there are things which you can do to make
progress as steadily as possible. There is also no beginning and
no end to this experience because wherever you reach, you
realise how much more there is. So start to notice everything
that you can.

## Keeping diaries

Keeping a record of your progress is a good idea. Diaries are
one of the best ways in which you can test your intuition from
day to day. This enables you to record and notice patterns of
experiences.

If you have an intuitive thought or some other type of
psychic experience, write it down and include the following
information:

◆ how it felt
◆ where in the body you experienced this sensation
◆ the time of day
◆ when and where you were
◆ what you were doing.

## Making decisions

Another part of living intuitively is being able to make
decisions more easily. Every day we make many little and some
big decisions. Some of these can change the course of our

whole lives. Making decisions, especially the big ones, can be one of the most useful areas for using intuition.

## Taking responsibility

However you make the decision, the outcome is your responsibility and you cannot blame it on anyone else. one of the most important aspects of taking decisions is accepting responsibility for its outcome, using it as an opportunity for learning more about yourself and others.

> There are no mistakes, there are only lessons to be learned.

## Noticing emotional changes

One of the nicest aspects of living intuitively is that your life will change in lots of subtle ways. The kinds of changes you can expect are:

◆ Fewer feelings of anxiety, fear or panic.
◆ A greater sense of security.
◆ Reassurance that things will work for the best even if it doesn't seem like that at the minute.
◆ A sense of calmness.
◆ Less likely to feel angry or irritated by little things.
◆ A greater sense of responsibility for your own life.
◆ A greater sense of personal agency or control over your own life.
◆ Less likely to be annoyed by other people.
◆ Less likely to be upset by other people's comments and attitudes.
◆ Able to make choices of response rather than reacting to situations and regretting it later.

Notice and record these little changes in yourself, however small. Be pleased with yourself for this new perspective developing in your life but do not be critical of yourself if you slip, remember that you are still learning and that learning will never stop. You will never know it all but the journey you live getting there is worth every second of it.

## Summary

Once we recognise time as a medium of experience rather than just as a measurement, we are able to respond more intuitively.

- ◆ Essential work for developing intuition is spending time allowing things to happen around you and noticing them all, focusing on each little incident, each little insect.
- ◆ Never dismiss anything as coincidence or just your imagination. Record all experiences and check to see if they come true in some way or another.
- ◆ Experimenting with your own awareness levels and experiences will create a stable and solid progress in your intuition development.

## Exercises

### *Exercise 1*

Start to include notes in your diary about how you feel at different times of the day and year:

- ◆ Experiment with sleeping at different times and waking to the sun by leaving curtains open in summer.
- ◆ How much more sleep do you need in winter, if at all?
- ◆ What happens if you use less electric light and allow your body to close down earlier?

Again, becoming more aware of the subtle experiences of our bodies will increase our perception and intuitive abilities.

### *Exercise 2*

Do you remember any occasions when you experienced something synchronistic, to do with a job, or a house, or someone else, or another area of your life, when you found that something which had been playing on your mind just came into your life? Record this in your workbook and make a record of all future experiences.

### *Exercise 3*

Think of a small incident that happened within the last two

days. It should be one which was mildly annoying at the time. Allow yourself to stay with the moment as if it is still happening now and explore it.

◆ What are you feeling?
◆ Where does this feeling occur in your body?
◆ If you had to point to this experience, where would the image of it be held?
◆ Is it pleasant or unpleasant?
◆ Would you choose to keep this feeling if you could?

Record your responses.

Now think of this event as something that happened a long time ago.

◆ Can you remember it?
◆ Is it still important?
◆ How do you feel about it now?
◆ Where do these feelings and memories lie, in or around your body?

Did the two different recollections of your event seem:

◆ Less significant?
◆ More significant?
◆ The same?

## Exercise 4

Using Figure 6 assess which type of time experience you have and how that affects you.

Now experiment with moving your time lines around and see how different positions feel to you – more or less comfortable, more or less open.

## Exercise 5

Start by thinking of several decisions which do not have significance in their outcomes. Choose your method of intuition for approaching this decision. Select whatever you feel comfortable working with and whichever seems the most appropriate for the decision being taken. Suggestions are:

◆ For simple yes/no answers, choose three tarot cards or the pendulum.

◆ For more reflective answers, use the *I Ching* or meditation.

◆ For choices, use timeline visualisation and 'see' the options in front of you before choosing.

◆ For dilemmas, use visualisations like the magic pool or use a wider spread of tarot cards to give more depth.

The only limitation is your own imagination and belief system.

# Choosing Your Approach with Mind Work

How well do you know your own mind? Do you ever find yourself in two minds? How many of your thoughts are you fully aware of? How often do you sit and watch your thoughts with interest? Or are you too caught up in their furious passage through your mind to really notice what they consist of?

What you think is what you get. I hope you have become open to this view of life by now, and more aware of how powerful this simple statement really is. How important it is to your own life experience! A thought holds its own energy, however slight or passing it is. The greater the thought, the more emotion behind it, the more creative it is. Emotion is the expression of our true beliefs and our heart's desires. But it is also the expression of our fears. All levels of thought are creative. Our lives are limited only by our own beliefs and fears. By using opening exercises to utilise your more creative attributes, you become receptive to all the little cues and hints which you previously overlooked in the haste of daily life. The more you get to know yourself, the more intuitive you become.

## Taking time to develop

- ◆ It is important to allow time to be quiet and to practise these exercises regularly.
- ◆ Some of these exercises are better done with a close and trusted friend who may be working along the same lines.
- ◆ Remember that each of you will have a very individual experience and there is no right or wrong way to open yourself up, so consider who the most appropriate person is you can work with.

- Always start any of these exercises with one of the breathing exercises given earlier in the book, you should have become quite practiced by now and feel the benefits of letting go through breathing.
- Chart your experiences and progress in your workbook. Writing everything down acts as a very deep trigger to your subconscious mind and assists your progress. It will also be interesting to look back and see how far you have developed.
- As with all things in life, trying to accomplish anything too quickly can leave you frustrated and with the impression that it is all a load of nonsense.
- Intuition is subtle and gentle, and will develop fully in its own time.

These techniques are powerful so developing them gradually is essential to get maximum benefit from them. It takes time to get to know yourself fully.

> I think somehow we learn who we are and then we live with that decision. (Eleanor Roosevelt)

## Learning about the self in quiet time

Having made several references to the speed and volume of stimuli hitting us every minute of our waking time, it seems appropriate now to address this situation. One of the most important things you can do is to listen to your own mind and the most reliable method of doing this is through meditation. There are many approaches to meditation and joining a group is an excellent approach. There are also many good books on the topic of meditation. But, simply speaking, meditation is:

- giving yourself time to slow down
- to contemplate yourself and life and the nature of existence
- to look at your thoughts and feelings and decide what they are telling you
- to look into your own inner heart and mind and become acquainted with yourself at much deeper levels instead of living on the surface all the time.

There are also several exercises at the end of this chapter and throughout this book which are forms of meditation you can try out. But the most important thing is to take time to listen to yourself in the quiet of your mind.

## Practising with NLP

NLP is the term used as a short form for Neuro Linguistic Programming, a model of learning and excellence in human performance. It was devised by Richard Bandler and John Grinder from observations they made of one the most effective therapists at the time, Milton Erikson. By watching his techniques they were able to ascertain his strategies which obtained such good results. NLP practices have now been developed to form a system of modelling for any behaviour that anyone else wants to do anywhere in the world.

## Applying NLP techniques

These are now being applied in every level of excellence. NLP is endlessly creative as a vehicle for change and growth, and it is up to the individual to utilise it as they wish. NLP is a sensory based system, it regards the senses as being the way we filter and create our own internal realities. Intuition is a recognition that the five senses are taking in far more information and are far more wide-ranging than we ever thought.

**Example:** You are standing in a crowded room and talking to a small group of people and having difficulty making yourself heard or hearing those close to you, when you are suddenly aware that your name has been mentioned across the room, yet you heard nothing of the rest of the conversation. This was first identified by Cherry and called the 'Cocktail Party effect'. This is an indication that your auditory range is actually ranging far and wide all the time and sorting information all the time but you are unaware of it until it flags you in some way. Intuition is when you receive a particular flag you then identify and verify as having been significant. Intuition is far more interesting as being a precognitive rather than a post-cognitive experience. Humans are pattern-making animals and as we like to make patterns, so we can make patterns out of the most extraordinary things. We tend unconsciously to programme our minds to notice certain things and to ignore others. This becomes our model, or pattern, for life. So we filter out information which appears to be irrelevant.

Reopening all these choices is part of becoming more intuitive.

## Precognitive intuition is knowing in advance

Intuition is totally useless if it is part of hindsight, perspective, or party talk, e.g. I had this dream. Acquire a conscious awareness of what intuition feels like. Precognitive experiences are happening all the time but we just don't notice them.

### *Shamanic human engineering project by Richard Bandler*

Bandler's interest in how far we can take magic has extended to all forms of society and cultural excellence. He currently sends people out to model, i.e. copy, shamanic healers in the Amazon. The researcher asks the healer how they know which plant to use. The healer says he goes to a particular clearing, thinks of the particular illness which he has to deal with, and asks the forest what to use. The forest presents him with an image of the plant or herb and he goes to find it. And he is really successful. The NLP observer then modelled the behaviours of the shamanic healer and asked for a herb for his own skin complaint. The forest gave him an image which he drew. The shaman said he knew and used it for skin complaints and cancers. Therefore the process is reproducible.

How did the forest know which plant to tell him to use? Maybe it isn't the forest but some database in the race unconscious, or in a supraconscious mind, that tells him what to use. We get back to the idea that if we can't explain why something works then we cannot trust it. Living spontaneously and intuitively is about trusting. If something works then use it. If you choose not to, what are you missing out on and what are you afraid of? That it might not work? Is that the worst possible thing? More likely you are afraid of saying you believe in something that other people may ridicule. Whose loss is it then? The 'why' questions are not really worth going into; they do work if you let them.

## Interpreting magic

The reason intuition and all these magical things work is because if people don't know any better, they don't know that it shouldn't work. The knowledge that such and such a thing can't happen is yet another example of the limiting thoughts creating a reality, which the human ego uses to prevent us from exploring further than we already know.

A little bit of knowledge is a dangerous thing because it tends to make us think we 'know it' and we clearly do not. Complete ignorance, or suspended knowledge and open acceptance of possibilities, are the only two states of mind which allow us to move on in this area. NLP works very much within the notion that anything is possible and does not accept the idea that it can't be done. If we can imagine it, we can do it. It might just take some time.

## Creating affirmations

Affirmations are a form of mindwork based on the principle that thought creates reality using the creative energy principle. By thinking something, we have created it, in light energy form at first. As we continue to send out positive and confident energies the reality we have created will occur in material form, in as long as it takes to materialise.

Other words for affirmations are:

◆ prayer
◆ desire
◆ wishes.

Affirmations are messages sent to the higher consciousness which create an intention in the mind. There are many books which show how to do this in detail, but a simplified explanation of how they work is to recognise that if we say something and believe it, two things will happen:

1  We send out the energy of our thoughts and wishes which create our reality.

2   We interpret our experiences in a favourable light for this to become reality.

| | |
|---|---|
| **Try it now** | **Affirming positively** |

Since this book is about living in greater harmony with yourself, some general self-development aspects are included. Some of the best affirmations we can make are positive ones about ourselves. Following are some that you could try. Say them to yourself in the mirror and repeat them regularly. Say them with a gentle, calm conviction of their truth. Desperation sends out a negative energy which will counteract the positive intentions of your affirmation.

◆ I am all that I can be.
◆ I am doing the best I can with what I know.
◆ All experiences are a good opportunity for me to learn a new lesson in life.
◆ I love myself and all that I am.
◆ I have all the love in my life that I need.
◆ I am learning to be my true self with each day.
◆ I forgive myself for being human and making mistakes.
◆ All my needs are met.
◆ I have all the friends that I need.

Now add some specific ones related to this book.
◆ I am very psychic/intuitive.
◆ Every day I am more self-aware and aware of everything around me.
◆ My life is calmer now that I am learning to trust my intuition.

Have fun making up your own. Make sure that they are all in the present tense and that you are not saying negatives like 'I do not want xyz in my life'. State what you do want, and state it loud and clear. Intend it to be true and it will become so.

## Ways of affirming

There are many ways of affirming:
◆ Say them out loud, either to yourself in the mirror or just from time to time throughout your day.

- Say them silently inside your head at regular intervals.
- Write them down and put them away, then get them out to look at from time to time.
- Write them out several times, like school lines – ten is a good number.
- Meditate on them.
- Sing them to yourself as you move around your home.
- Ask friends to confirm them in a group or one-to-one.

You can use affirmations for the following:
- improving your self-esteem
- improving your self-confidence
- losing/gaining weight
- developing skills and abilities
- staying healthy
- releasing anger and energy blocks
- creating your own ideals in career, relationships, material needs, financial needs, home/house, studying/learning new skills.
- and anything else you can think of that you might want to change in your life.

Make sure your affirmations will not affect another person adversely. If you want a promotion then make sure that the person whose position you want is also promoted or goes on to something else for their highest possible good. If you want a skill make sure you use it wisely and for the greater good. You cannot use affirmations to get you out of difficult or challenging situations, because these are your lessons in life, but you can use them to release the negative emotions and events that have occurred and create something better next time. You can use affirmations to turn them into a positive experience through changing your perceptual stance.

## Developing assertiveness

Being assertive is being able to state your feelings and get what you want out of life without losing control, or being controlling of, or controlled by, others or by situations. It is also about releasing the fear we have of ourselves and allowing us to be our true selves. To do this we need first to know who we really are and what we want to be assertive about.

Assertiveness is not about getting our own way, it is about living in harmony with everything and everyone around us and allowing each individual to be themselves in their own way.

Assertiveness goes hand in hand with acceptance. To achieve this we first have to know ourselves very well. From that we can gain quiet strength. This enables us to accept everything that occurs, and to make our own choices about how to respond so that we get what we want, too.

For instance, if something uncomfortable happens, we can choose how to deal with it.

◆ We can become angry, which might be the intention behind the originator of that experience and so we are being controlled.

◆ We might choose to side-step the issues and carry on doing our own thing, which is being assertive and self-contained.

Most assertiveness training emphasises working on how to deal with a situation, and learning new styles of communication. This section of the book will take a different approach. Using affirmations you can:

◆ Decide what you want.

◆ Invite that into your life, quietly and confidently.

◆ Assess the difference between what you really want and what you think you want.

◆ Relax and trust that whatever you most wish for will come if you make room for it. By relaxing about situations you are more likely to get what you want.

◆ Learn to approach life in a more open way and automatically experience less stress.

## Relaxing into the work

Flowing with your own natural ultradian rhythm, the natural cycle of brain activity levels that continue throughout the day and night on a roughly 90-minute basis, find a slump time or dreamy time to try Exercise 2. The dreamy times are when our right cerebral cortex is functioning most effectively. This is where we find our imagination, creativity and intuitive functions operate best.

This is one of the most beneficial times of the day for relaxing and making the most of your creativity. Your brain is actually working very well but it is the part of it that does not like to think or work. It is the part of your brain that wants to play and create. And most of all – to stop thinking. If you can make this into a routine you will find it very beneficial.

## Learning how to create

Creative visualisation works on the premise that you must first become more aware of who you are, then what you do and believe, and from this comes the ability to have what you want in your life. Choose an aspect of your life that you would like to change, adapt or develop:

- ◆ work
- ◆ self-esteem
- ◆ friendship
- ◆ relationships
- ◆ home
- ◆ health
- ◆ abundance (in any area, e.g. money, comfort, sense of physical well-being).

It can be a good idea to develop these skills on smaller things in your life because learning how to get it right is part of the 'getting it better in the future' process. It helps to build trust and understanding of how all this works if you start on small things that are easier to accomplish, and work upwards.

Appreciate all you have already. Emphasising what we have is often a good way of acknowledging the positive in our lives and not overlooking it in the search for more of whatever we think we need to make us feel better.

- ◆ What is good and what is not so good?
- ◆ What have both these aspects taught you, given that nothing in your life is without a positive intention behind it?

Making spidergrams of this is a good way of approaching this. Use your work book for creating these.

## Stage 1: *What do I really want?*

So you have decided what you really want. Now break it down into what that represents in your life. For instance, do you want more money?

◆ What does money represent – status, respect, security?

◆ What does this give you that you don't already have?

◆ Is this the best way to meet that need?

This stage is important because if you do not decide exactly what it is you want, then you're likely to create something you think you want and then find that this is not bringing the satisfaction you expected. Taking time and care over each stage helps you to learn more about yourself and create your own life.

Remember that there are no mistakes, only lessons to be learned, so if you do get it wrong this time then take a different approach. Learn from your mistakes, they are the richest resource you have for getting it right next time, better than any books or workshops you can do.

> Be very clear and very consistent about what you want. Do not say you want this thing in your life, and then say you don't really just in case it doesn't happen.

Hedging bets is not being creative or trusting. What is important is to recognise that what we want may come clothed in another format to the one we expected. We cannot control the manner of delivery of our wishes. Leave them free to come as they will, for our highest possible good. There is nothing you can't have as long as it does not come at the expense of anyone else, e.g. promotion at work must be because someone else has gone on to something better for them.

## Stage 2: *What I believe – rejecting limitation*

This is about what we believe we are entitled to have. How often do we think, feel or say 'There's no point in my wanting this because it won't ever happen'? It won't with that attitude.

That is called resistance. We have many resistance voices in our heads which tell us we do not deserve this, it is not acceptable to want that, we are selfish or greedy. These are the voices of limitation. Since we create our own reality and always get what we ask for, if we want something but believe we cannot have it for whatever reason, then we cannot have it. It is as simple as that but not for the reasons we first think. So give yourself reasons that you will be allowed to have your wish come true. For instance, if you want a new love in your life, consider:

(a) What it is you actually want from this – companionship, passion, security, etc.?

(b) What are your beliefs are about love. Does it last, is it good to have new lovers or is it promiscuous; can they be trusted or can you trust yourself; will they hold you back or work to support you as you will them etc.?

(c) Are you afraid of having a new partner in your life – what might they confront you with that you are unable to cope with, what secrets might you have to reveal to them?

(d) What do you think about other people with partners – are they stuck in ruts, lucky, free, tied down?

(e) What are the advantages of not having this change in your life, what would the change require you to give up that you cherish?

(f) What benefit would this bring to others around you, what are the ripple effects? With each of these six 'spiders' take time to allow the thoughts to come through. Is it what you really feel? Until you work that out you cannot create, you are blocking it.

## Stage 3: Unblocking your creativity

The next step is to release your blockages and this can be done through the use of affirmations, meditations and expressed desired intentions. For instance, as all negative thought and feeling has its roots in fear, we should try to analyse the cause of the fear.

Fear is: False Evidence Appearing Real.

A simple affirmation will do. Write your own because this is more meaningful to you, but some ideas are:

◆ I am a loved and loving person.
◆ I release all fear.
◆ I invite new love to come into my life.
◆ I am open to love, loving another unconditionally, and being loved unconditionally in return.

Affirmations are more powerful if they are said out loud to yourself. Speaking into a mirror increases this further. Do it with serious intent, albeit allowing for a fun element as well. Who wouldn't have a bit of a giggle talking to themselves very seriously in the mirror? One way of having fun with an affirmation is to play with it; try to clap it into a clapping song against your own hands in the mirror. Then you are using four senses, sight, sound, touch and hearing. This has the effect of firmly creating the image and intention with both sides of the brain – the ego-based logical left brain and the intuitive, creative right side. If you add a feel-good fun factor it should lodge in your limbic system too, the emotional brain.

Are there any parts of you that are still objecting to your wishes coming true? Do you feel quite comfortable with this or is there still a doubting part? These objectors are actually trying to protect you, but they may well be coming from your ego (loosely termed Earth Guide Only), and we are talking about being creative from our higher, inner selves, or our spiritual selves, whatever term you are comfortable with. So it is our higher selves that we need to consult for this wish to come true.

### Stage 4: The time to ask for help

Meeting the higher self can be achieved through meditation and self-hypnosis. There are several formats which help you to do this. Ask the Magic Pool (see Chapter 12) to transform your fears. Another very powerful way is from shamanic traditions. It is relating to the first level of incarnation to which we are still attached through the minerals in our body. First find a stone which you like the look of; this can be any stone which you find lying around. Tell it your desires and fears, blocks and beliefs, about what you want in your life and thank the stone for accepting the responsibility of helping you. Then bury it in some soil, preferably in a garden, to release the energy you have given the stone through your words, back into the very essence of the planet and its powerful forces of creative energy and nature.

However you want to view this ritual, it is another way of confirming to yourself that you wish to release your negative feelings and become more in touch with yourself. It works. It could be explained in many terms – the self-fulfilling prophesy and other psychological paradigms – but we are not concerned with how it works at this stage.

## Stage 5: Seeing the new

This stage asks you to create the image of yourself having achieved your wish come true. Close your eyes and create the image in your mind's eye. Using self-hypnosis or any trance, dream-like state will increase the effectiveness of this energy. This form of visualisation comes from NLP and is called future pacing. See yourself in *x* number of weeks/months with your wish in place. See every aspect of it in full. This way you can check to see if it is what you really want. Using a dreamy state is one of the best ways to achieve this. Now get enthusiastic about this, enjoy it, laugh with it, love it and immerse yourself in the joy of having your heart's desire fulfilled. Use all your senses, hear, feel, smell, touch and taste it all. Know it inside out, experience it from all angles.

Do not get into desperation with this. Your happiness must never depend on anything; you must be able to be content with life as it is presented, and this is how to get what you want. Your higher self will tell you very clearly that you can be happy without this desire being fulfilled and will teach you this lesson again and again until you learn it.

## Stage 6: Releasing the old to make room for the new

We cannot continually add new things to our lives without making way for them. This exercise relates back to Stage 2 section (e). You will have to acknowledge what this change will cause you to give up. The past and all that we have been is one of the richest resources we can have in life. It is the composite of us as we are now and offers the greatest opportunity for growth. Using your time line now, go back and see what you have come through and already learned. One of the most important perspectives for self-healing and self-development is to recognise that nothing which has ever happened was intended to hurt you. It was all intended to teach you and to lead you closer to your true self.

Releasing the past can only be done in its own time. Rushing it removes the chance of extracting all the learning from it, it is avoidance and denies us our own inheritance. So we will go through the same things again and again in different ways and formats until we have got it. Until we are released from the past we are not open to receive the future. Are you able to cope with being happy?

### Stage 7: Receiving the new

Stage 7 requires you to meditate and ask for guidance from your higher self again. This is in preparation for you to receive your new life in all its fullness. Send out an affirmation that you wish to receive guidance on making way and receiving the new. Whatever you are told to do should be completed as instructed. This can often come in the form of dreams, or again from deep meditative states. You may be asked to go through a kind of ceremony which symbolises your acceptance of the new into your life. Sometimes this involves taking a walk, making something symbolic, planting something in a garden to signify new growth, etc. Whatever you are to do will be shown at the right time, provided you have fully completed all the previous stages and not fudged any of them. The final step of this is to trust that, having completed all aspects of creating your new life experience, you will receive it. Without trust it is pointless, since it is the conscious intent which makes it self-fulfilling. If you find it hard to trust fully then remain ambivalent. However, any form of cynicism or rejection will create a negative force field and your dream will recede even further, fulfilling your prophesy of expected failure.

Since this chapter contains specific techniques, a closing thought for meditation is included.

> What risks are there in freedom compared to the choices of captivity? We can remain in fear or we can break free. It is our choice.

## Exercises

### Exercise 1

In order to develop intuition using an NLP model, the following strategy is most effective.

#### Step 1
◆ Decide what it is you want to intuit and what intuition means to you (refer back to Chapter 1).
◆ Ask how you know 'that is an intuitive experience'.
◆ List in sensory specific terms how you knew, what exactly you felt: make an as rich as possible sensory specific list or pattern:
1   Is it warm or hot?
2   Do you see, smell, taste or hear?
3   Does it move?
4   Where do you feel it?
5   What triggered it off?
6   What is replicated in other experiences you have had?
7   How would you identify this if it was happening again, keeping it as sensory specific as possible?

Remember that all these experiences are subjective. Making a note of each of these aspects should help you begin to realise how much you miss of what goes on around you. We all do it – even psychics or intuitives miss things, but less than non-intuitive people.

#### Step 2
This next step is an interesting one that reinforces your new skills. Simply using your imagination, create a new past for

yourself, one in which you have always been psychic or intuitive, when you have always had these skills and you have just got to remind yourself of them. You can even write down what you have always been able to do and have fun with this. Be creative, remember the only limitation is your own imagination and belief system.

## Exercise 2

Work with a partner and play a game of 'I'm Your Temp for a Day'. This involves telling your partner all that they would need to know in order to take your place and do all that you do for a day. You should of course make it specific to intuitive experiences only for this, otherwise it would take forever. Tell your Temp the first thing they need to know – not when or why, but how they would know and how they would know that they are expanding on those experiences. Again, creating access clues for yourself to use can be both fun and very rewarding. For instance you can close your eyes and tell your stomach to feel in a particular way when you are being clairvoyant or intuitive. Keep the instructions specific and again identify things like heat, colour, size, shape, sensation, even smell.

## Exercise 3

Taking a brain break. This exercise is about getting you to experience things which you  can choose to incorporate into your daily life. Make sure that you have at least 15–20 minutes and will not be disturbed. If you do this when you are at work, arrange to take a short break. It will make you more effective later on.

Take a deep breath and allow yourself to drift away. Make a conscious note to allow yourself to come back to full awareness within your allocated time and then trust that you will do this. If you are uncertain then set a small alarm to bring you back. Do not attempt to time it consciously or you will be working against this mind state. Let your mind wander where it wants to go.

This is drift dreaming, letting the mind wander where it chooses and observe the thoughts as if from an external position. If you find yourself concentrating on a certain problem or issue, just tell your mind that you will deal with this when you are in a different frame of mind. It is essential to be able to monitor your thought patterns in order to master them and become self-controlled rather than controlled by them. Then you can start to add creative visualisations.

*Intuition is reading the energy of connections between all things.*

# Understanding Energy

T his chapter addresses the concept of energy from two perspectives of philosophy:

◆ Logic (reasoning questions) using mathematical models to describe the logical sequences of ideas.

◆ Metaphysics – which addresses questions of existence.

For many people there seems to be a need for some kind of proof of the concepts explored in this book. You can have the proof of your own experiences and you can have theoretical proof from science. Of course there is no proof that will satisfy those who do not wish to be convinced and cynicism is a very effective form of defence against new ideas which challenge current ways of understanding our daily existence.

## Tackling new ideas

New ideas are threatening and challenging and can create uncertainty. Yet new ideas are the basis of all the changes in human society which brought us from caves to where we are now. Change is inevitable.

> Great spirits have always found violent opposition from mediocre minds. The latter cannot understand it when a man does not thoughtlessly submit to hereditary prejudices but honestly and courageously uses his intelligence.
>
> (Albert Einstein)

All major scientific discoveries have struggled against resistance to change and many significant discoveries effectively cost their discoverers their lives, Copernicus and Galileo to name but two. Galileo was put under house arrest in 1633 until he died in 1642 because he refused to obey the Roman Church's demand that he refute the idea that the sun was centre of the solar system, not the earth. He was officially pardoned by the Pope in 1979, over 300 years from the original condemnation of his beliefs.

Copernicus had earlier written of the possibility and it was suggested as far back as Aristarchus in 310–230 BC. We do not now question the rightness of these discoveries and laugh at the lack of vision of those who did not accept them in their own time. It is highly likely that we are now capable of making the same mistakes with new ideas. History shows us how much we fail to learn from experience generally.

### Resisting change

It is the resistance to change, including changing ideas of life, which causes the difficulty. That resistance is based on the fear that what we already know and believe may be wrong. The fear that:

◆ if there is more to life, then we humans are not in control
◆ and if we are not in control then who is
◆ and if we do not know who is in control how can we trust or be certain of anything
◆ and what does 'being in control' mean, and so on.

Humans have a tremendous propensity to fear quite irrational things. Living intuitively means living in tune with yourself so that you do not experience unnecessary fear.

> So let me assert my firm belief that the only thing we have to fear is fear itself.
>
> (Franklin D Roosevelt)

### Identifying the universe

We live on a minuscule planet located in a place called the universe. To be in something you must also be of it. It cannot be otherwise. Everything is part of the universe and therefore everything is connected to everything else. The confusion is caused by an illusion of separation according to our human perception. We tend to overlook, deny or dismiss things we cannot see or understand. We do not choose to recognise that everything is connected and we believe that this is then true. But logic shows us that it cannot be so. Our belief in our separation makes it true for us in our perception, but not in reality.

> A human being is part of the whole called by us the universe, a part limited in time and space. We experience ourselves, our thoughts and feelings as something separate from the rest. A kind of optical delusion of consciousness.
>
> (Albert Einstein)

### Understanding the nature of illusion

Things appear to be separate from us. Other people are not connected to us physically as Siamese or conjoined twins are, but they are connected to us through the planet, through the air we breathe which has been inside someone else's lungs a while ago. When someone leaves the room or our life, they appear to be separate from us, but they are not in reality – they are just further away from us. And they are made from the universal energy as we all are, as everything is. It is merely arranged differently so that we appear unique and different – like a tree and grass. Yet if broken down, ultimately everything contains the same components.

We are all connected in other ways too. For example, through race consciousness, and the commonality of humanhood, or our shared home on this planet and in this universe, etc. The scientific principle of connectedness is the basis for most of this chapter.

◆ Space is the universal substance of which everything that exists is made.

◆ Energy is the organising power of the substance, i.e. it is the shapes that substance forms, that connects everything to everything else.

◆ It is the reading of these energies that is the basis of intuition or psychic abilities, however you wish to term it.

◆ It is the connectedness of everything through the energy which allows us to read through time i.e. into the past and future, as well as 'see' and 'know' things in the present at a distance i.e. through remote viewing and telepathy and other phenomena.

The most exciting thing to me is that this is the part where science, religion and philosophy all start to say the same thing. For one theory presented in the first edition of this book, it was less than a year since the evidence was completed and presented to the scientific community. Three years later, as I wrote this, I heard on breakfast news this idea being considered and taken seriously.

## Labelling energy

Different terms for this universal energy are:

◆ Spirit.
◆ God.
◆ God Energy.
◆ The Universal Energy.
◆ The Holy Trinity.
◆ The Oneness.

You can see by the terms listed, that this is not a minor influence in history. Hence this subject is of enormous controversy and every opinion will also contain the personal agenda of the researcher or theorist involved because:

1. No matter how much they claim to be impartial, no scientist can be because they need to have a presumption or a hypothesis before they can begin to plan how to prove it.

2. Each one in their own field can never see the whole. However much or however little they are aware of this, they will want their theory to be 'right'.

My own agenda in this is that I want the God/Energy principle to be right because since I have increasingly worked in this and with this throughout my life, I have found a peace that I never knew existed before. In one sense I don't mind if I am wrong because it's so good I shall keep doing it anyway. What better reason is there anyway? Does one need any more reason than that?

## Understanding mathematical principles

Wilf Leng follows the traditions of all the great scientific leaders and pioneers, including Einstein, Faraday etc. He intuitively knew the answer to his question of how the universe works and what Einstein missed, five years before he was able to support it mathematically. Although the actual mathematical process which he demonstrates to the higher echelons of the scientific community is far beyond the scope of this book and my own comprehension, the following point summarises the basic premise:

◆ that the universe is made of a creative energy which is quite impartial and only knows itself because it is all that exists.

### *Building on Einstein*

Initially Leng and his team looked at Einstein's theory of relativity. Einstein's contributions to science in the early part of the twentieth century were based on his attitude of more or less ignoring the scientific thinking at the time, especially to break free from Newton's laws, which he did by failing to learn them at school.

> My intellectual development was retarded, as a result of which I began to wonder about space and time only when I had already grown up.
>
> (Albert Einstein)

This allowed him greater intellectual freedom to think originally and relatively. Remember Mark in Chapter 2? One of the greatest problems in our education system is that it no longer teaches people how to think, merely what to think. Those who choose their own way are often labelled deviant or difficult – even failures – but they often turn out to be the most successful in later life, the innovators and entrepreneurs of our time.

### *Original ideas beginning*

Einstein's PhD thesis in 1905 examined the movement of particles. He looked at three types of particle:

1  sugar molecules in water solution – calculating their size accurately for the first time

2   dust particles suspended in air – as they zigzag in sunlight called Brownian motion

3   light particles and the differing amount of energy carried by different colours of light.

All these phenomena were explained by activity or movements around the particles affecting them. For instance the dust particles 'dance' because they are bombarded by particles of water and air, the irregularity of which creates the erratic zigzag movements. Light particles, called photons, knocked out the electrons from the metal surface or light filament, and the brighter beam just had more photons in it.

So the energy of the electrons 'knocked out' is equal to the energy of the photon which 'knocked' it and the size of a zigzag dance for dust is equal to the size of the particle of air or water bombarding it. (Cause and effect.)

He also established the idea that entities of energy can appear both as waves (like ripples on a pond) and particles (like dancing dust) i.e. wave particle duality, in subatomic worlds. For instance, subatomic particles are not limited to being one thing, they are creatively adaptable.

## Einstein, time and space

After several attempts to prove Newton wrong, Einstein's theory was eventually accepted as correct. By then he had already moved on to examine the behaviour of light and electrodynamics of objects in movement. This is the beginning of relativity. It is called a special theory because it is concerned only with objects moving relatively, in straight lines and at constant speeds. It challenged Newton's Law because it suggested that time could appear to shrink or grow according to an object's speed relative to some other object. Yet subjectively we know this to be true in our life. How often do you find time flies or drags relative to your perceptions?

Einstein backed all this up with rigorous mathematical evidence. Thus the speed of light is constant regardless of any external movement from the source or from the observer. He then realised that this meant there was a connection between mass and energy, making them equivalent to each other. Thus the famous equation

$$E=mc^2 \text{ or } (energy)= (matter)(speed \text{ of } light)^2$$

Although ignored initially, eventually the importance of this equation was seen and other people including Einstein's old professor started to publish papers about it.

Later Einstein had a daydream wherein he recognised that a person falling through air could not be hurt nor feel their weight because the acceleration cancelled out the weight which is felt through gravity. Thus he could extend relativity to include gravity and acceleration (curved lines and changing speeds) as well as straight lines and constant speeds. It took Einstein eight years to demonstrate his initial idea which he gained intuitively but this intuition changed the nature of science as it was then known. This story illustrates and explains the true power potential of intuition, and demonstrates why our own resistance to change must be recognised and addressed.

## Understanding relativity

A good descriptive way of understanding relativity is the behaviour of a beam of light within a falling item such as a box. If the box is free falling, the beam of light would cross it in a straight line, but it would appear to be bending or curving as it dips to keep up with acceleration, caused by gravity pulling the particles of light and thus bending the light beam. It's rather like a sheet of lycra being stretched out flat and ball bearings being rolled around on the surface causing it to dip and hollow around the movement of the ball bearings. The ballbearings represent the beam of light. Heavier ballbearings would affect the path of smaller ones, causing them to roll into the bigger dent. The faster it moves, the longer it takes to fall into the bigger dent and the more straight the line of its roll will be, although it is always a bent or curving line to some degree. To summarise, the presence of matter informs space of its curves and the curved space informs matter of its movement.

Leng took this idea one step further and pointed out that if something continues to curve, eventually it makes a circle curving in on itself. Leng called this endless curving 'winding'.

'Winding' is the crucial first key to understanding the nature of energy being endlessly creative and all that really exists.

## Taking Einstein's concept further

Einstein's student, David Bohm, began to open up the idea of non-locality as a strange aspect of quantum reality. An atomic nucleus simultaneously releases two particles called an electron and a positron, in opposite directions. It is impossible to decide which is which until it has interacted with something, then it can be identified and its counterpart likewise identified. But until it has interacted it could be either. It exists in either state, and therefore does not become an electron or a positron until it has been measured as such. This gives it a limitless creative potential to become whatever it becomes.

But how does the particle travelling in the opposite direction know that it is now the opposite. For instance, the electron has been identified so therefore the other now knows it is a positron? How does it know how to behave?

This is probably one of the most important aspects of this scientific explanation of intuition. If quantum particles can intuitively know what their opposite 'partner' is doing and respond accordingly – then we can also do this as humans. This indicates a consciousness at subatomic levels of matter. So tree huggers and rock meditations suddenly have real scientific implications. So does prayer and the central principle behind much of this book – that thought creates reality.

## The psychic internet

This is called non-locality and we will come back to it specifically later in the chapter – but this book is based on the principle of non-locality in practice which I believe is true intuition. This is exciting to me personally, and I intuitively understand quantum physics without having had any teaching in the subject before exploring this approach with Wilf. It suggests a communication across time and space which occurs at an instant. This was demonstrated to be true in the 1980s using photons but even now we are still not recognising generally the full implications of the phenomenon.

## Explaining the power of three

This is the second key principle behind Leng's theory and is based on Euler's (pronounced Oiler) formula of connections between points and lines, of which everything is composed. Euler's pathways are called *closed connected pathways*, i.e. they are created in one movement (of the pen). The basis of intuition is that everything is already connected, so intuition is the reading of those connections.

### *Making closed connected pathways*

Try joining up the following sets of points without lifting the pen from the paper, so that every point is connected to each other once and no connections are crossing.

Fig. 7. Connecting the points.

Could you manage to connect up any of them following the instructions? It is not possible except with the group of three. In fact for group (ii) I cannot join up every point and can only manage most of them. I can join a-b, b-c, c-d, c-a, and b-d but not a-d without unclosing the form. One connection is not made.

Key:
—— can do this in one movement
– – can't do this in one movement

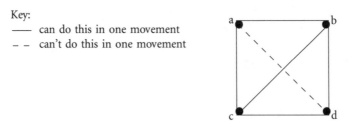

Fig. 8. Connecting four points.

I can only connect (iii) by lifting the pen from the paper. Have another look before you move on.

So from any one point, if you have an interaction going out along any connections then to keep together (not dissipate or be divided up) it can only go to three next points. If it went to four one of the connections would *unclose* (open) the connections of all four. This would not keep the interaction together. Joining five points can only be done by lifting the pen from the paper once, and leaving two points unconnected.

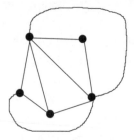

Fig. 9. Connecting five points.

What Euler also noticed was that here was a continuous relationship between the number of points (N.), the arcs connecting them (A), and the number of spaces or regions (R.) connected to the figure, including the area outside or around it. The examples below may help you to see what I mean.

|  | N − | A + | R = | 2 |
|---|---|---|---|---|
| Figure i | 3 | 3 | 2 | |
| Figure ii | 5 | 9 | 6 | |
| Figure iii | 4 | 5 | 3 | |

## Adding a third dimension

The Euler formula explains the power of three in a two-dimensional sense but we live in a three dimensional world. Leng took the three points and connected them with a further point which touches all three, making a tetrahedron or three sided pyramid.

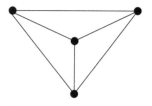

Fig 10. Leng's three point 3D connection.

This explains the power of three in any supposed dimensional world. Any dimensions is always forced to 3D (next 3 points in any one direction sense) if a closed interaction is to be achieved. The tetrahedron shape itself is not so important (it's odd to stack together). The three mutually nextness of a non-dissipative interaction is important because it is stable and doesn't break up. From any origin you go into a three-form shape but not necessarily a tetrahedron – there's a bit of elasticity needed here to create the variety.

If you start to connect these tetrahedrons you get an infinite creation of incredible stability. This is the quality which is essential for a universe in which matter is stable, i.e. not forever changing from moment to moment, but which has the potential to do so gradually. The key point here is that it is not the connections but the points themselves which are the basis of all matter. These winding 'points' (Einstein's bend continued all the way round) are the basis for movement and the diversity of matter which we are able to experience at all levels. These 'points' are the basis for energy, or the composition of energy.

## Summarising properties of 'points'

The mathematical explanations of the universe and cosmology have shown the following key factors:

- ◆ Everything that exists is structured by the transmission of universal energy.
- ◆ Universal energy is transmitted via the existence of infinitesimally small points which are continually spinning or 'winding' on themselves.
- ◆ The transmission is at the speed of light.
- ◆ The winding (spin) multiplied by any orbiting and multiplied by any change (another sort of winding) is the speed of light.
- ◆ The winding itself depends on the way the next points all around are winding.

Everything that exists is always moving at the speed of light, even an object that appears static, because the electrons which spin (wind) around each atom are moving at the speed of light. Yet something which is in motion as we observe it will have the electrons moving at a lesser speed. But a calculation which combines the two kinds of movement will show that it is collectively the speed of light Thus:

- ◆ The transmission of energy creates movement which is endless and constant.
- ◆ The points are arranged in sets of three 'next' any origin, in any one sense (direction) from that origin.
- ◆ This means that, as they are all connected (next) to each other, information is relayed throughout all the universe in only three directions at the same place, hence 3-D-ness. However, because the points are next to each other, they all interact. This means that they all pull each other or influence the movement of each other – like the ballbearings on the sheet of Iycra.

## *Seeing in three dimensions*

If you are looking at an image of a tree, that image is not just coming from one direction but from every direction possible and is being bounced or transmitted around the whole universe before coming back to you. Your perception is that it comes from one direction only because that is how the human brain translates the information.

**Case Study:**

Some people are able to visualise like this, my own son included. He can hold an image in his mind's eye and observe it from every angle and position possible. He can also enlarge and reduce it in size within his own mind. He also experiences certain musical rhythms as patterns of energy inside his mind and can sense their patterning in a way that most people would not be able to understand. This is similar to the rhythmic music of many ceremonial chants and dance music and it instils a sense of wonderment and oneness which he finds hard to explain but makes him feel more content and complete in himself than at any other time. This is his intuitive experience beyond the reality of the material world.

## Analysing properties of energy

This section is broken down to make the progression of ideas more accessible to all of us who are not naturals with quantum physics and maths but would still like to have some understanding of the science behind these ideas.

We have established that energy is creative and that the spinning or winding points give this energy a structure. Each point controls the others around it equally, and is in turn controlled by its neighbouring points. This controlling nature creates patterns of energy:

a)  Radiation – which is the transmission of the energy. We see it as light or feel it as heat.

b)  Matter – which is the energy in solid, liquid, gas or plasma forms that we can actually see. Matter or form, gives the energy stability in zero-, one-, two- or three-dimensional form (e.g. plasma, gas, liquid, solid in chemical structure).

◆ Energy orders the winding of the points to create the patterns.

◆ Energy comes from outside and shows space there and time there, but is not inside, not of itself.

◆ The energy is in the space and changes it by being transmitted by the windings of the points.

◆ This change we call the lapse of time.

◆ Energy is the start of universal logic, which is the form of the universe, the primitive thing that starts it all off.

◆ It is completely primitive in itself and it can't all dissipate at once. So it is spread around because the points are next to, and therefore hold each other up as well as set each other going. That is, the ones going set the others going, and the ones holding up try to hold up the doing ones.

◆ There is infinite energy in space. Infinite must start at one point and follow finite patterns, i.e. stability.

◆ There are one-, two-, or three-dimensions spinning particles (the fundamental particles) but it is the nextness of the winding points which restricts energy from doing infinite things at once.

There are no intervals in these points, they are packed together and space is continuous so interacting could only go point to point. So continuous three-ness appears.

- Each point can join to all others and form a fourth point in a tetrahedron or a three-sided pyramid structure.
- It is possible always to join the three points but you can never do this with four or more and two is two-dimensional so not applicable to matter.
- An Euler path is a *continuous and closed path*, four points can be either continuously connected or closed but never both.

So by working on the power of three, the closed continuity of the universe never breaks, it forms a finite number and shape and there is no way out.

## Maintaining stability

The nextness mustn't break for maintaining the continuity of interaction and matter, otherwise interactions and fundamental structure would start to fall apart and dissipate. The dimensionality of three prevents this happening. This is called 'neat' or 'transparent' proof of the theory. This is the quality which allows us to believe in any kind or permanence but also to recognise that the permanence is an illusion.

Matter can never be created or destroyed, only transformed, so the creativity of universal energy is in the infinite ways in which it can manifest itself.

## Explaining energy metaphysically

Metaphysics is the study of theories of being and looks at:
- What exists?
- What is its nature?

It has three branches.
1  Ontology – categorising that which exists.
2  Cosmology – studying our connections with the rest of the universe.
3  Other matters – such as topics to do with the existence of God and immortality, mind-body relationships such as free will and determinism, appearance and reality, and concepts of time and space.

The power of three reflects in all the ancient beliefs as:

◆ The Holy Trinity: Father, Son and Holy Ghost.
◆ Mind/Body/Spirit
◆ The three jewels of Buddhism, i.e the Buddha, the *dharma* (teachings) and *sangha* (community).
◆ The triads of Sephiroth, the tree of life of the Kabbalah from Judaism.
◆ The Trimarti – the three aspects of god in Hinduism.
◆ The three stages of pagan womanhood – maiden, mother and hag.

If we use the term God as the basis of energy in its intelligent and creative nature, we understand that god is divided into three and that this reflects the nature of the universe itself. The Science of Mind metaphysical church, sees God as the life Principle, a limitless creative power.

◆ **God the Father** – the supreme thinker – thought creates reality. We tap into this aspect of god energy when we create our own realities through our own thoughts – space with its strict logic. The space (universe) out of which everything is made (shaped) by the energy.
◆ **God the Son** – the son is the mind the universal unconscious and the law of mind or the laws of the universe such as cause and effect (karma), the transformative power of love and the law of grace which allows us to change and move on.
◆ **God the Holy Ghost** – the energy that causes the shapes in the logic of the universe and the human dimensions of experience. The concrete world that humans accept as reality and the experiences that are of this reality including the journey to transcend it. Holy Ghost is the body and all manifestation in material and experiential world all human material experience/effects.

Another way of looking at this is to take the three dimensions of humanity and relate to them. Some people find this more comfortable than using terms such as God since there are so many emotional connections and taboos associated with the God word for many people.

◆ Spirit: thought and intelligence above humanity consciousness. The representation of God thought in our higher selves or our consciousness.
◆ Mind: the universal unconscious, the human intellect and emotional challenges.
◆ Body – all manifestation and material experiences of energy. The condition of human physical experience, with the emotions and physical challenges to overcome.

## Mistaking reality

The error in human consciousness is to assume that the material experience is all there is. In fact it is only an aspect of a much greater reality expressing itself. The parent mind – father I AM – the individualization of parent mind is us – in us is the god eternal I AM in wherever we find it.

Most traditional science is based on the idea that there are hard and fast rules which prove reality Yet these rules are being shown to be less than concrete and much of science is coming up against ideas which are crumbling under evidence that there is something more powerful which can change everything. This power is the power of consciousness or thought and it comes in many forms:
◆ prayer
◆ wishes and dreams
◆ affirmations
◆ willed intentions and desires
◆ beliefs and accepted knowledge
◆ ideologies
◆ fantasies and imagination
◆ the constant inner 'self talk'.

## Intuition, illness and healing

The most remarkable breakthroughs in evidence have been scientifically researched and summarised by Larry Dossey in his book *Healing Words*. He discusses the creative power of thoughts, as prayer, in bringing about healing. He points out the following stages of consciousness in attitudes to healing:

1  The materialistic approach that the body is a machine and you repair the parts, not the whole, that everything is cause and effect and mind is not a factor. Includes acupuncture, herbal medicine, drugs and surgery.
2  The acceptance of mind/body influences and the relationship between them in both causing, and healing of, illness and disease. Includes counselling, hypnotherapy and imagery based alternatives in conjunction with biological techniques.
3  Transpersonal medicine, i.e. mind is a factor but not only the mind of the ill person. It is the mind of all humanity and the belief through the collective unconscious which both causes and heals illness and disease. Prayer, reiki, shamanic and metaphysical healing comes in this form of approach. It accepts that there is a 'mind which goes beyond the individual consciousness'. This allows 'non-local' healing at a distance, and also healing through time.

## Understanding non-locality

This third concept brings into play the idea of non-locality, i.e. the mind is not confined to one place or time. We already know that we can experience feelings of past, present and future all at the same time. We also know that everything in the universe is connected, and that matter can know something of itself and of others when travelling away from each other.

Most of the testing on the application of this approach of healing has been done using medically accepted methods of double blind conditions. This means that when the experiment is carried out, neither the researchers nor the subjects know who is in the experimental group and who is in the control group.

A control group creates a base line from which to measure the difference between a non-prayer group and the experimental 'prayer' group. Within the research on prayer healing, the following points have been found:

◆ Distance between healer and healed is not a factor.
◆ Desperation reduces the effectiveness of healing – the thoughts of the patient being a stronger influence than the thoughts of the healers – thought creating reality for the patient whose desperation reflects their lack of trust.

- Recognition of positive aspects of the condition increase healing, i.e. what is the gold nugget of learning inside all experiences.
- Prayer has 20 per cent effectiveness in healing illness. This statistic is as good as any form of drug therapy could be expected to be. No single drug can heal all illness. This is also based on the strength of all consciousness factors influencing each subject being healed.
- It is possible to diagnose illness from distance, using energy readings, before the illness can be diagnosed traditionally (see Myss in Further Reading, also the chapter on aura and chakras).
- It is possible to heal the actual illness before the prayer is carried out.
- The surrender of the will to a higher source and acceptance that the consequences are for the best possible good increase the likelihood of healing.
- The beliefs of other people can influence our own health, for example, they can create illness as well as heal i.e our perceptions/ judgements of others as being sick, etc.
- The individual's unconscious mind plays just as important a part as their conscious mind.

To quote Dossey: 'Our understanding of the relationship between spirituality and healing is vastly incomplete. We should admit the obvious. *There is a great mystery here*... something unknowable and essentially beyond human understanding'.

## Summary

Universal energy is everything that exists, including the creative energy potential required for us to think and learn about energy as a concept.

- Energy is a key concept that we might find difficult to grasp because it is so vast, so beyond human experience, and yet we can experience it personally.
- Energy connects everything to everything else.
- Science is gradually enabling demonstrations of energy using maths as illustrator.
- Intuition is reading this energy in all its formats.

- Universal energy is generated from the power of mind; both the human and universal mind.
- Energy has the power to heal and cannot be anything other than as it is, it cannot be destroyed or created but can be transformed – the basis of immortality.
- Intuition means reading the energy.
- Prayers, thoughts, beliefs, etc. are continually influencing things through the connectedness of everything – the basis of evolution.

CHAPTER 9

# Opening Your Mind

T his chapter looks at two further areas of our mind:
   ◆ the difference between belief and knowing
   ◆ evidence and trust.

Understanding how these aspects of our mind work and relate to each other is another essential part of knowing yourself and, therefore, 'knowing' what is happening around you and being intuitive.

## Believing is not knowing – or is it?

The intellectual arguments both for and against much of what has been put forward so far, are based on suppositions of what is and what is not. Many people hold these ideas as beliefs rather than what they really are, which is ideas.

All ideas have evidence of one sort or another to support them. The difference between a belief and knowing is the weight you place on that evidence, where the evidence comes from and what it means to you.

### Case Study: Susan's Intuition

Susan sensed that Dave had been lying to her. She didn't know how she sensed it or 'knew' and started to look for evidence to support her intuition. She obtained one or two items which, to her, confirmed her belief. Now she knew. Susan then confronted Dave with her knowledge and showed him the supporting evidence. He immediately gave alternative explanations for her evidence and told her that her belief was wrong and that she did not know anything of any truth. Susan doubted her knowledge and her intuition and gave Dave the benefit of the doubt on the surface but continued to collect evidence for her own belief. Eventually she decided she was right and, although she could not prove her knowledge, she ended the relationship. Essentially trust had evaporated between them and she realised it was the trust which mattered, not who was wrong and who was right. That had become irrelevant._____

### Knowing through trust

The case study shows that trust is a crucial part of knowing and believing something. Does that only apply in interpersonal situations? No, it applies in everything. Scientists for years trusted that Einstein was right and taught his theories as fact. yet other scientists, whilst respecting Einstein's work greatly, looked for more evidence to support it or refute it. They did not stop at knowing, they still tested the idea as one of great worth but merely that.

A belief is an idea which has sufficient evidence to support it for acceptance, but one person's need for evidence may be quite different from another's. This includes both the *type* of evidence and the *volume*. A subjective experience may convince the subject, but when described to another may be treated with derision as being of any use as evidence.

### Solipsism

Solipsism is the theory that the only possible knowledge is that of oneself and, therefore, subjective experience is the only evidence for that knowledge. Most of this century has seen western society adopting an anti-solipsism attitude. This does not make it true or not true, merely a current trend in thinking.

> Solipsism is a very valuable approach to life because it allows for subjective experience, a return to a way of thinking that values personal experience and places responsibility for yourself firmly back in your own hands.

Subjective experience is the basis of 'knowing' and turns either an intellectually or an emotionally held belief into knowledge by uniting it with the missing aspects of self. Thus it becomes the whole experience of the individual.

As discussed in the chapter on energy, this is as common a phenomenon in science as it is in personal life and is the basis for all aspects of human progress. If we ever accept anything as total belief or knowledge without continuing to question it, we are denying the need to look and explore further in our lives. What we know may be wrong or right, what matters is that we continue to explore it. We should learn from Galileo's experiences. Most of our knowledge and beliefs are also based on emotional perceptual positions which we have been taught or chosen or adopted, either unconsciously or consciously. Trust is a big part of this.

## Recognising emotional/intellectual blocks

If we have been taught to fear our intuition then we will also fear ourselves because our intuition is a deeper part of self than linear, logical thinking. There is nothing against left brain logic, we all use it often and with great effect, but we have a whole brain so let's start using it all and see what we can really do.

Trust, or rather not trusting, is a very big block to overcome. It can be disguised as:

◆ cynicism
◆ over-critical analysis leading to total rejection
◆ a desperate and insistent need to know 'why', without considering divergent ideas and answers
◆ contempt
◆ dismissal
◆ reducing it to no more than a party game or a topic for curiosity but not for serious consideration
◆ making fun and openly ridiculing the ideas and experiences.

As you continue to work on developing your intuition it is essential to recognise:

◆ What you are really thinking and feeling about everything you have read so far.
◆ What your previous experiences have been.

All these will affect your ability to open up.

---

**Try it now**  Look back at previous chapters and think about some of the information offered. How did you react to it? Did you:

(a) believe it completely?

(b) disbelieve it completely?

(c) hold belief in suspension until more information is obtained?

---

The answer you gave in the exercise will tell you a little more about how much we all block ideas that challenge our existing beliefs. But if we only accept what we are told and never keep open to anything else then we will never make progress as a species. It was the ability to imagine, and then to believe in 'anything is possible' that allowed us to move out of caves. There is never enough information to convince someone who does not want to be convinced.

## Examining belief systems

Whatever our background, if we are not using our intuition fully already but feel that we would like to or that something is missing, then the chances are that, like Mark in Chapter 2, we were taught not to trust this part of our intelligence. Intuition is a very important part of intelligence and is the basis for some of the most remarkable business accomplishments and scientific advances that have ever occurred. So why is intuition seen as unscientific and not to be trusted? And why are we made to feel uneasy about people who openly use it?

Belief systems develop from and manifest through many different forms:

◆ materialism and scientific realism
◆ religion
◆ education
◆ social norms and expectations
◆ cultural patterns and differences.

## Materialism

This view of life is based on perspectives of modern science, specifically classical physics, which originates with Descartes and Newton. Materialism suggests that you should not believe in anything without proof or evidence, and preferably evidence that can be quantified or measured in some way. Most psychic or intuitive experiences cannot be easily quantified because they are subjective. Increasingly evidence is being acquired using very recently developed approaches, and is overwhelmingly in support but largely ignored. This is for several reasons:

- ◆ it challenges existing patterns of thought
- ◆ it confronts existing power systems
- ◆ it undermines the status and position of people who are not involved in it
- ◆ it creates uncertainty in what we think we already know.

Materialism states that it wants scientific evidence yet it is unscientific for one simple reason:
- ◆ It does not allow for new possibilities that do not follow on from existing assumptions.

For this reason materialism immediately limits us because we have already shown that imagination is the basis for all that has developed in humankind. It is non-scientific and limits what is allowed to be discovered or understood. Therefore it is based on fear.

True science always changes to incorporate new discoveries and keeps a completely open mind. It knows that any fact can be challenged and accepts that constant change is the reality of all experiences and that change could mean anything.

## How materialism impoverishes

Materialism has also impoverished western society in a way that clearly shows why it is limiting. It suggests that security and happiness are also based on materialism, yet western society has high records of individual unhappiness demonstrated through:
- ◆ numbers of divorces
- ◆ levels of child abuse
- ◆ increasing suicide rates
- ◆ increased use of drugs for depression
- ◆ increasing violence and theft, including state management
- ◆ increasingly violence used to enforce social rules and laws.

## Separation from the oneness

Science and the needs of the spirit are seen to be quite separate aspects of humanity, yet if each of us is one whole person no aspects can be separate. This compartmentalisation of self and experience is also part of the lack of self-knowledge, and in metaphysical terms is called separation from the oneness.

The turn against materialism is growing. In spite of materialism many people still hang on to spiritual beliefs through church and other forms of worship. New approaches to beliefs are being sought, and fundamental movements are also growing because of the desire to find some kind of firm spiritual basis for living. The result is a crisis of confused life beliefs and desires, unnoticed needs crying out to be met and a wake of social disaster. The need for some kind of total belief system to cling to is an indication of the fundamental insecurity of lack of inner self-awareness.

## Religion

Most religions and denominations teach avoidance of people who profess to have powers of insight. Conventional Christianity especially teaches that clairvoyancy and spirit work such as tarot is the work of the devil, and to be feared and mistrusted. Modern attitudes seek even to deny anything that is not of the material world. Yet some priests do have knowledge for performing exorcisms. If any religion argues that god is in everything and everywhere, as most do, then nothing can exist except that which is of god. God cannot be restricted to a set of rules and told what is/is not of god. Even what we could call evil is of god because it is an opportunity for us to learn from mistakes if we choose to look.

We never learn from history and we continue to repeat. This is the same on an individual level. We are shown continual lessons of how to be and how not to be. God is teaching us in the only way possible, through experience. It is us who call some experiences evil, so that we do not need to take responsibility for their existence and learn from them on every level.

### Protecting a mistake

Most religions forget to say it is not wrong to trust your own knowledge or skills. Clairvoyancy is a skill which a few unscrupulous practitioners use to manipulate others to their own will. This is a negative use of intuition and will ultimately cause damage to the individual doing it, but a few vulnerable people might get hurt along the way.

◆ Vulnerable people need to learn to trust their own intuition and not be easily led. They can only do this through experience, and therefore the 'cons' are providing valuable lessons.

◆ If you are in tune with your own intuition you will sense a con and avoid it. Religious leaders may be well intentioned in teaching avoidance of clairvoyance but it leaves many people unable to protect themselves and fearful, making them more open to attracting negative experiences.

## Education

The whole education system teaches us to think and experience everything in a linear, logical, measurable way. It is easier for teachers to measure success in a linear format. For instance many children have an intuitive feel for numbers and mathematics, coming from deep within. They may be penalised for working this way and told to do it again, showing their calculations. When asked to explain how they knew the answer they may be accused of cheating or copying it from someone else. Intuition is not considered.

These experiences are common to many children. They are examples of an intuitive knowing (of numbers) which they have been taught is 'wrong', not to trust. Some children find it very hard to work in any other way and are labelled slow/ difficult learners because they do not work in the linear way. yet many masters used intuition first and then used all kinds of thought processes to support it.

Einstein always remarked on how valuable his intuition was and how he knew the answers before he knew how to get there. By having the destination in sight he was able to make the journey and come up with the theory of relativity.

## Social conformity

One of the challenges of being very psychic or having a personally developed spirituality in your approach to life is that you are seen as different by other people. This is because your emotional energy vibrations are at a different level from other people's and they can unconsciously find this challenging. They have a sense of not being able to get to know you. Sometimes there is a sense of intrinsic strength or a presence about you that other people feel in awe of, and it is difficult for them to use the normal methods of control or manipulation to get what they want from you.

The answer to this is based in a society which fears anything it cannot control, manipulate or explain away. We are pressured into being the same as everyone else. Many of the great innovators throughout history also had a difficult time socially. If people have conformed to the social norm and ignored their psychic abilities, they have chosen to be less than themselves as a whole person. But because of that desire for social normality they are unaware of exactly what is missing and will seek experiences from the social norm to support them in their denial.

## Cultural differences

The diversity of human cultures allows us to see how much more intuitively some people live than others. For instance, many North American Natives will 'know' in advance if someone, even a complete stranger, is going to visit them and will prepare a meal in readiness. Other cultures such as the Tlingits, an Inuit tribe, when close to death, give each other signs by which they will be recognised when they return in a new incarnation. They also place emphasis on dreams, especially those of children and pregnant women, as having prophetic powers.

If a culture accepts and even exalts such skills, people who have them will be free to explore and express their gifts and abilities and develop them further for the greater good of all. The individual must learn to trust:

- themselves and their judgments
- their abilities to deal with what life offers
- their ability to remain true to themselves.

## Learning how to trust

Trust is the art of letting go of any sense of a need to control one's life, allowing oneself to live with the moment, to deal with whatever comes along and when it occurs.

Trust is generally called going with the flow. It does not mean ignoring the past or the future, but not dwelling on them for more than the instant it requires to assess the present.

### Case Study: Susan and Dave

Dave had been flirting with Susan on and off for nearly two years. She found him really attractive and sometimes hard to work with. They had spent time together and the relationship had become sexual, but whenever she wanted to take it further Dave came up with a good excuse why he couldn't, usually to do with her personality as he saw it. On the surface they had a lot in common and enjoyed several evenings together. Eventually she pulled away from Dave and decided that they could remain friends.

The day before he went on holiday with another girlfriend, he phoned Susan and told her that he really wanted to be with her and could they talk when he got back. Her intuition told her not to agree to this. She heard it as a voice in her head and also as a twist in the belly. Her intellect told her that this was what she had been wanting for a long time and she should at least see how it went. The voice told her he would hurt her. In spite of this intuition Susan agreed and waited for his return. They met and went out and the relationship became very concentrated immediately, with talk of children, commitment, etc.

Susan's body did all it could to tell her to back out. She became very tense, unable to sleep, especially when he was with her. He criticised her over everything, even things which she knew far more about than he did. He would not allow her to express herself or shine in any way, yet told her how much talent she had. After a few weeks Dave told her that she was too uptight and ended the relationship. Susan felt very bitter and hurt. She lost a lot of self-confidence and was quite low for some weeks. What had her intuition told her!

In the case study Susan was offered a valuable lesson and in the end it was a positive experience because she learned from it. If she had trusted her inner knowing and what her body was trying to tell her, she would have saved herself a painful lesson. It is unlikely she will make the same mistake again. Will you?

## Trusting against the evidence

Intuition requires us to trust things against our own intellectual evaluation of the evidence. Belief systems ask us to believe in god, or something else, yet for some people there is not enough evidence to put our trust or faith into that belief. Trust at this level requires us to let go of our own limited understanding of reality and allow ourselves to be taken to another level, usually with the promise of greater riches or levels of inner peace and happiness.

This is the point where some people turn from much of what a book like this suggests. They feel that learning to trust yourself wholly is just mumbo jumbo and life is the way it is so don't trust. If you think like this, has it also occurred to you that you might be wrong? You might break the social rules and stop being a conformer.

People's happiness and quality of life tend to increase when they become more trusting. But they are only deluding themselves, you might say. If they are happy in their delusion and you are less happy in your reality, then who is more reasonable in their approach to life? Ask yourself:

♦ Why are you so afraid of being happy?
♦ Why do you spend your whole life wishing you could be?
♦ Why do you spend your life looking for things outside yourself to make you happy?

Since all happiness comes from within and never from outside of us, it must be a personal choice. We have to take that leap of faith and learn to trust in order to find what that happiness really is. Until we take the leap of faith, we cannot know what it is like in our own experience.

**Case Study: A Cliffhanger**

Mike is stuck on a ledge of a cliff having lost his footing and fallen. The rescue teams have assessed the situation and have decided how best to approach the situation. They have a good view of all the possibilities and the previous experience of many similar rescues. Mike is aware that the rock above him seems very crumbly and is falling on him from time to time. He wants to try to climb down the cliff. He cannot see what is below him but feels such a fear of falling that he wants to reduce his height on the cliff. The rescuers explain that he must work his way back up the cliff and they will send down a rope to help him. He catches the rope and decides to trust their advice even though all the evidence and his own fear tell him to go the other way. He is rescued and later sees what the rescuers saw that he could not have seen from his position on the cliff. That the tide is coming in and he would have been swept away.

## *Beginning to trust*

The example in the case study is a metaphor for learning to trust ourselves fully, to become more self-aware. It often seems far too dangerous and complicated from where we are, but if we wish to be rescued, to find our true selves, then we have to begin to trust who that true self really is. And we usually have to begin by trusting others who have made that same journey. The evidence you need is in their quality of life experience. This is not so much what happens but how they feel about it, not how you would feel about it from your position stuck halfway down a cliff face.

This is exactly the same kind of situation we are faced with when we are asked to trust and let go of our fears and begin to live intuitively. We want to climb back down the cliff rather than go up and believe that the evidence we have is correct. The problem with trust such as this is that you cannot know the evidence until you have climbed the cliff and seen it for yourself. You can only see it when you look back down and see what those who have trusted have seen and already know.

## Summary

Opening our mind and keeping it open can seem like a full-time occupation but eventually it becomes second nature.

- In order to fully develop our intuition we have to become aware of our influences.
- Discovering what and how you believe and know is an essential step in the process.
- Learning to trust and being prepared to listen with open mind and heart will achieve more than adherence to existing patterns of thought.
- The evidence for trusting is available if you choose to accept it.

## Exercises

### *Exercise 1*

In your workbook write a short paragraph on how you feel about each of the following:

◆ intuition
◆ psychic abilities
◆ god
◆ dreams
◆ meditations
◆ tarot cards and
◆ other psychic tools such as crystals, *I Ching*.

Now write an extension of the above, under these headings:
(a) What experience do I have of this?
(b) What were my parents' attitudes to this?
(c) What evidence do I have to support the validity of this?

Most of us have had experiences in the past which we could describe as psychic, but perhaps have dismissed as coincidence. Exploring all this evidence and experience from the past is essential. Now complete the following questions in your workbook:

◆ What were the attitudes of those around me when I did express having a psychic experience?
◆ What religious background and teaching do I have?
◆ What experiences do I have of being or feeling different to others?
◆ How much did I adapt myself to fit in, for the sake of being 'one of the crowd'?

The more work you do on yourself here the easier it will be to open yourself up to your intuition.

### *Exercise 2*

Spend some time thinking through each of these questions before answering them and make sure you are fully aware of the depth of each question.

- How much do you trust yourself?
- In which areas of your self and your life do you trust yourself the most?
- In which areas of your life do you trust yourself the least?
- How much do you trust other people around you?
- What are the limitations you put on trusting yourself and others?

(E.g. I only trust people when I have known them for a long time. I only trust myself when I have asked someone else for their opinion to confirm mine.)

## Exercise 3

Write a list of times when you had a hunch or an intuition, and followed it or didn't.

1  What happened, was it right or not? What happened in the end?

2  Write a list of times when you did not listen to your intuition and went against it for a more logical reason.

3  Write a list of times when you did follow your intuition. What happened in the end?

CHAPTER 10

# Working with Subtle Energies

Subtle energies surround our bodies and sustain us through daily life in the physical plane. They protect us both physically and emotionally. Someone who is confident and comfortable with themselves will have a strong energy field. A nervous breakdown is a breakdown in these energies, leaving us with no protection. The energies we will be looking at more closely are:

◆ chakras

◆ the aura

◆ colour energies.

These energies are very much part of our daily interaction with other people. They contain the energies of our state of mind, our emotions and thoughts. Sensitive people can pick up the emotions and feelings of others easily and can feel drained very easily by negative experiences. Some people feel exhausting to be with and others just plain uncomfortable to be close to. If these people come too close we want to move away, yet another person does not make us feel like this at all. We can often tell who has come up behind us even if we do not see them because we can sense their familiar energy field and welcome it into our own. This originates from the minute electrical current which runs through the entire nervous system, carrying sensory data around our body and into the spinal column and brain. These energy fields travel out from us endlessly but we will concentrate on the closer energy fields, illustrated in Figure 11.

## Tuning in to the chakras

*Chakra* is the name given to seven energy centres that are located down and through your body. Each one corresponds to

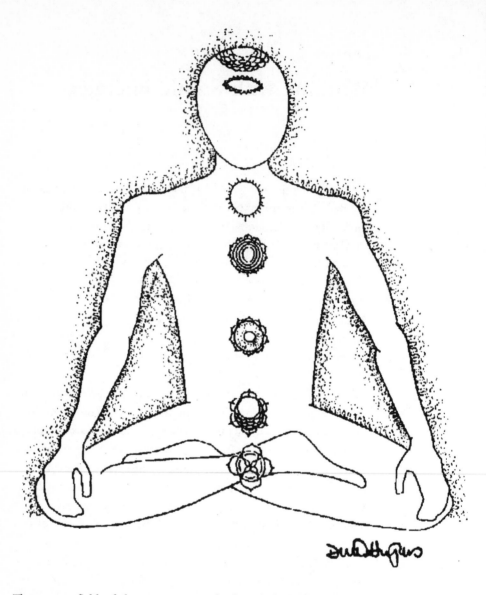

The energy field of the aura surrounds the whole body and looks like small flames dancing from the surface, in layers moving outward detectable for up to two feet or more, in decreasing intensity. The chakras are symbolised with different designs, each with its relevant number of closing petals, for conserving power within the body. The crown chakra is depicted here showing advanced enlightenment because it has grown larger than the others and is beginning to cover the head. The Buddha is often shown with great curls of the crown chakra cascading down his head and also a knot rising from the centre like a bun, towards the universe/enlightenment.

Fig. 11. The subtle energies of the body.

a different area of your experience. A chakra is a whirling energy force which runs through from front to back of the body. Each one comprises a force field within our body, roughly like the kind of patterns which iron filings make when sprinkled onto a piece of paper with a magnet underneath. Mostly we cannot see our chakras, but can learn to be aware of and use their energy in creative and positive ways. The chakras relate to the energy vibration of different colours. They are a good monitor of general health and can become blocked by certain types of living styles and experiences.

The chakras are located all over the body, but the main ones are found in an almost straight line going up the trunk from the base of our spine to the top of our heads.

The term chakra means wheel in Sanskrit. Chakras are discussed extensively in Sanskrit and Tantric literature, as well as having been adopted by several other societies including the Rosecrucians, Freemasons and Theosophists. Carl Jung called them centres of consciousness.

## Sensing the chakras

Have you clamped your hand to your forehead in realisation that you already knew something just told to you? Have you needed to sit down after hearing some shocking news? Have you doubled over in pain at the words someone has used against you? Have you felt a very warm, heavy feeling just below your navel when you are in the presence of someone to whom you are very sexually attracted or involved with? Most of us have. Do you use or recognise the expression 'giving your heart to others' when you are reaching out to someone else in a positive way? Do you fold your arms in front of you when you are facing someone with whom you do not feel empathy? Does your throat close up when you are upset or find difficulty expressing yourself? All this is evidence that, although you are possibly not aware of it, your chakras are being affected.

Chakras overloaded with negative emotions become blocked and closed down. If we are very needy, they become jammed open, and we begin losing energy in damaging ways which can easily lead to health problems.

### Recognising the rainbow warrior

The chakras relate to the colours of the rainbow and this is the basis for the term rainbow warrior which relates to man's relationship with these living energies of the universe. The name was adopted by Greenpeace for their boat which patrolled environmentally sensitive areas of the planet, specifically trying to block the release of huge amounts of negative energy in the form of nuclear testing and environmental damage.

### The first chakra

The root chakra is predominantly red and is your connection with the earth, the experience of feeling in touch with yourself and safe in your environment. See if you feel more comfortable sitting on the floor, or on grass and earth, instead of having concrete and human constructions of intervention between our bodies and our planet. Wearing different shades of red can help us to feel more confident and able to cope with whatever life throws at us. Different reds have different influences on energy and confidence. If you feel unstable, have difficulty settling anywhere but feel a need for security, it is likely that this chakra is blocked. You should be able to feel secure wherever you are on the planet, it is all your home.

### The second chakra

The second chakra, called the spleen chakra, vibrates to orange. It is largely to do with our sexuality and certainly where we feel sexual desire most strongly. It responds to the vitality of the sun and makes us feel better after lying or being in the sunshine, lifting our spirits and making us feel much more positive. People who are uncomfortable with their sexuality are often blocked in this chakra. It relates to our personal power and a sense of achievement. It represents our family and tribal connections.

### The base chakras

The first two chakras together are the base chakras and relate to our sense of contact with the planet, our tribal home, in terms of responding to the energy and creative forces, including growth and reproduction. They are connected to the energy of *kundalini*, the fire serpent in our spines. When all the chakras are balanced, *kundalini* is released. It is experienced as an ecstatic rush of energy up our spine and all over our body, impossible to describe but unmistakable when experienced.

## The third chakra

The third chakra is over the solar plexus and vibrates to yellow. It forms the centre of our sense of self, our emotions and feelings, and is the cause of strong sensations seeming 'like a punch in the stomach'. It is a very important energy centre in relation to how we feel about ourselves. Problems with indigestion and stomach upsets indicate blockages in your ability to deal with emotions sent in your direction by other people, and your whole sense of identity and purpose.

## The fourth chakra

The fourth chakra is the heart chakra and vibrates to green. The heart chakra is where we respond to others in a giving way, our loving concern for others and our environment or home. It is common for people in difficult situations to experience pains in the chest, showing the heart chakra is blocked. 'Open hearted' people are generally complete and content in themselves. They don't find it hard to accept and forgive others. Most heart attacks occur on Monday mornings – a sign of broken hearts being forced to continue until they break down.

## The fifth chakra

The fifth chakra is the throat chakra, our self-expression and communication. It vibrates to blues and turquoise. People who suffer from a lot of sore throats will often have difficulty in expressing themselves as they would wish, either because they are unable to articulate themselves or because they are not heard when they do. It is our ability to express ourself and tell our truth with integrity and without fear of rejection.

### The middle chakras

These three chakras – third, fourth, fifth – correspond to our conscious and self-awareness. It is important to use our skills and knowledge of these forces in order to improve our day-to-day experiences, especially those related to other people. By opening our chakras we can improve our ability to communicate honestly and openly, to share positive emotions, giving love to others and accepting their love for us. Closing these chakras when faced with unpleasant situations means you are less adversely affected by hostile others.

### The sixth chakra

The brow, or third eye, chakra is our intuition and foresight. It is linked to psychic awareness and the deeper levels of understanding which come from within our unconscious minds. It is the source of our most deep and instinctive thoughts. It responds well to deep, dark blue colours and indigo. Blockages in this chakra usually take the form of difficulty in thinking and perceiving the options for the future, and a lack of general forethought and intuition. These are skills which get us through much of our life since we rarely 'know' what will happen but we can intuit it. Migraine is a common indication of blockage in the brow chakra and our denial of psychic abilities.

### The seventh chakra

The crown chakra is our link with the universe, which we often forget we are part of, and is over our heads all the time. It is closely linked with the fontanel and explains why this is still open in new babies. The usual explanation given, that it makes room for the bones of the skull to expand to accommodate the growing brain, is rather inadequate when you consider how much growth the bones in a limb will achieve between birth and physical maturity. It is predominantly violet but incorporates many other colours in a rainbow prismatic effect. It is the channel of receiving energy and intuition but it can also, through development, become a radiating centre. Images of the Buddha shown with his head covered with curls which peak up over his fontanel is a representation of his crown chakra and depicts how it is reaching up into the highest realms of spiritual awareness, up into the heavens or universe. It represents the energy that continuously rises up through humans from the earth and into the universe beyond. Christian symbolism also shows the crown chakra as the crowns worn by the 24 elders being continuously cast down in front of the throne of god.

## The higher chakras

The two higher chakras relate to our higher, spiritual experiences as humans.

## Cleansing the chakras

For all chakras to be working properly it is essential for the individual to be fully balanced in their life and to have a sense of harmony with their own inner thoughts. It is possible to cleanse and unblock chakras through visualisations and by working on your inner health, self-love and development.

Through working with the chakras, we can develop the ability to be consciously aware of the effects other people are having on us, and we can choose how we will respond rather than being hooked into interactions we later regret. Being able to protect and open ourselves at will is an essential aspect of developing intuition because we learn to read the energies coming towards us.

## Sensing auras

The aura is the energy field which surrounds our whole body and is the basis of our protection and sense of personal space. Research into how people react when they are too closely packed together reveals that those who do not have the degree of physical space around them which makes them feel comfortable, create the mental space by ignoring others. This is effectively withdrawing our energies into the chakras and closing them. Have you ever noticed how much people avoid looking at the person next to them in a crowded train or tube, yet their bodies are very close to each other? We need to feel our sense of space around us and we feel this through the aura. Research carried out by Felipe and Sommer (1966) showed how this was accepted when it is seen that there is no choice – the place is crowded – but if there is no reason it becomes a source of antagonism and resentment. Sommer *et al.* chose female students sitting in a library at tables where there were at least two empty chairs on either side of the subject. The experimenter sat closest to the subject. Subjects did one of several actions to establish their territory: they put a bag between them, moved their own chair a little further away or even moved seat altogether.

## Recognising layers

There are several explanations for the layers of space we sense around us. Research by Hall identified four layers:

◆ intimate distance: 0–18 inches and may involve actual bodily contact
◆ casual personal distance: 18–48 inches reserved for close friends and people we trust
◆ social consultative distance: 4–12 ft reserved for colleagues and formal contacts
◆ public distance: 12 ft and beyond for large meetings, talks and general formal settings.

Kirlian photography has identified the existence of the energy fields. It takes clear photographs of the aura through using a different kind of sensitivity rather like infrared sensors on cameras that can 'see at night' These different energy fields are illustrated in Figure 11.

Einstein viewed the human body as a multi-dimensional organism comprising physical systems formed from cells which are in dynamic, constantly changing interaction with each other and which create complex energy fields. No single cell is ever motionless, no single atom is without movement. The belief we have in solid matter is related to how tightly packed these particles are, and the energy they emit is related to the energy resulting from their vibrational friction, the energy from the particles rubbing against each other.

## Energy attacks

Some people can make us feel devastated. Some experiences do the same, leaving us hollowed out and drained. People who have so little of their own positive energy act like energy leeches or vampires, absorbing your positive vibrations and emissions into their own field. They will feel much better after spending time with you and will seek you out if you do not close your energy down to them. Closing the chakras and being consciously aware are the best protections you can have. If it is a particular situation which you cannot avoid, exercise 3 is a very good form of protection. It utilises all the colours of the spectrum combined, which makes white.

All forms of emotional shock and trauma are aura-shredders. So are strong fear-based emotions such as anger, jealousy and dishonesty. The energy used to deal with these emotions will drain the aura and leave little energy for living life to the full. That is why it is so important to heal negative emotions and release anger. You do very little for the person with whom you are angry and their well being is their responsibility not yours. You do it for yourself and for your own protection.

## Reading auras and colours

Most of the time we are unaware of reading each others' colours and do not 'tune in'. Occasionally we might be aware of a slight glow surrounding some people, especially the head and shoulders. This will be particularly visible after meditation or contemplative work on the self.

Just as light has particular frequencies, matter does too. The higher the frequency of vibration, the less dense or more subtle the matter. The etheric body or aura is a result of these higher frequency energies. We call them subtle because, rather like gaseous substances they cannot be easily seen, but we know they are there because we could not live without air to breathe.

Damaged auras can be seen as if they have tears and rips in them, and areas of black and grey where it is almost destroyed. Areas of strong red can mean anger, but red can also mean active energy and security. Orange is creative and sexual, yellow is emotional, green is loving, blue is communication, indigo is intuition from the third eye and violet is celestial connection or spirituality. Combinations of colours can sometimes be seen like flames coming from parts of the body and each layer of the aura interplays with the next. The more you relax and allow your focus to slip, the more likely you are to see auras and eventually colours. You may sense colours intuitively rather than see them.

## Meditating with colours

There are a number of ways in which we can use colour to enhance our lives and improve our general health. Choosing colours to live with in our homes is a very personal thing and can be the cause of argument between couples who feel they need different colour schemes. We are drawn to colours that most reflect our inner life. Once we become consciously aware of energies we can choose colours to work with and heal ourselves.

### Wearing colours

The clothes we wear are significant in enhancing our sense of well-being and there are new approaches to choosing which shades and tones of colour to wear to most enhance our appearance. Beyond that we can use colour to enhance a specific quality, for instance wear a lot of strong red when you wish to be assertive and blues to communicate well. This may be the whole colour scheme or it may just be a scarf around the neck. Experimenting with these ideas is the only way to find how they work for you.

### Riding through the rainbow

Below is a guided visualisation which you can put onto a tape for yourself and use at any time, and which combines all the colours and their qualities.

*With your eyes closed, picture yourself floating high above the earth drifting and dreaming, floating through patches of fleecy white clouds, just after a sudden spring shower. Feel yourself drifting on now, slowly and gently, on and on until you come to a beautiful rainbow, shimmering brightly before you, with shades of hearty red, creamy peach, golden yellow, cool mint green, aqua blue, midnight indigo and dusky violet. You think how pleasant it would be to drift on through the rainbow, experiencing the colours one by one – and changing direction ever so slightly. You prepare to do just that, starting first with the band of hearty red. Feel the band of red beginning to enter the soles of your feet, carrying with it a warm glow of strength and power which spreads quickly up through the calves of your legs and on up through the rest of your body, flooding every fibre and nerve with a warm rosy glow of energy, strength and power. Breathe deeply and slowly, as you continue on through the band of red, and inhale the colour and the feelings that go with it. Let yourself experience them fully and completely, as you breathe them in and saturate yourself in their warmth.*

*As you continue slowly drifting on, the band of creamy peach begins to penetrate the soles of your feet and spreads itself throughout your body in just the same way as did the red, bringing with it an increasingly beautiful sensation of complete and perfect peace. As this peacefulness progresses on throughout your body, it blends with the energy which you already feel making you serenely more aware of everything you experience.*

*Next the golden yellow band begins to spread itself throughout your being, filling and flooding you with its delicious golden glow, and bringing to your consciousness an ever-increasing sense of happiness and well-being. Flow with it and breathe it in, as you allow yourself to merge completely with this wave of radiant happiness. Blend with it so completely that you begin to radiate back an answering happiness of your own.*

*You are entering the green band now, as you begin to experience a wave of pure refreshing joy, carrying you ever higher, as you feel yourself being inundated by endless sensations of indescribable joy and bliss. Rapture and ecstasy, wonder and delight, breathe it in, blend with it and savour the delicious emotions which are being added now to all of the other feelings you have gathered in your journey through the rainbow and which you still retain.*

*Now you are beginning to draw in the colour of aqua blue which causes you to feel as free and as fluid as the aqua waters themselves. Feel yourself blending with all the water everywhere on the planet, rushing over the surface of the earth as her banks caress you, moving over the rocks and soft river beds, plunging down cliffs to form waterfalls in a headlong rush to the sea. You are again drawn up to the sky and back to the rainbow and the light blue band once more, ready to enter the darkening blue ethers of midnight, and the tranquillity and mystery of night. Feel the darkness surrounding you and allowing you to become more aware through your other senses as the colours fade into darkness. The indigo feeling caresses your spirit deeply, nurturing and healing you.*

*This band is thinner than the others and you quickly start to float out into the light once more, as the darkness turns to a beautiful violet band. It fills you silently with a sense of freedom to an infinite degree, for now you feel that you are able to step behind all your everyday thoughts and all your customary roles. You slowly drift to a stop within the violet band and you are filled with the stillness and peace of a warm, mimosa-scented summer night. You can feel within your own being the beautiful, tranquil colour of the violet sky, long after the sun has slipped down behind the horizon.*

*While you remain here within this violet band of light, in the hyperemperic trance which you have entered, the suggestions which you receive will help to guide you into new pathways of awareness and new dimensions of being, richer and more rewarding than those you have known before.*

All types of meditation reveal more of our true selves to us and these guided meditations or trance journeys are very effective in developing the skills of allowing our imagination to work fully for our own benefit. This is discussed in greater detail in the following chapters.

## Summary

Recognising your energies permits a greater level of self-knowledge and balance of intuition.

- ◆ The energies of the body are part of our protection and we must use them accordingly.
- ◆ Colours vibrate with different frequencies which reflect different emotional states and energy levels.
- ◆ The aura represents an extension around our physical body of which we are very much aware.

- ◆ Different people are allowed different degrees of proximity in our aura.
- ◆ Developing methods of self-protection is essential if we are opening ourselves up to psychic experiences and intuition.

## Exercises

### *Exercise 1 – Opening and closing chakras at will*

Each chakra can be opened or closed down at will. With practice this is easily achieved. The chakras are covered by a folding mechanism, rather like the petals of a flower opening and closing. By visualising this opening and closing process, we become more balanced with our feelings and experiences.

Sit quietly and focus on each chakra in turn, starting at the root chakra first. Visualise it as a swirling vortex of energy flowing through your body from back to front. Be aware of the colours of each chakra, perhaps visualising them as flowers. You can even choose a flower to represent each one for your own use, for instance the red field poppy for the root chakra. It is better for you to choose your own representation and work with it regularly, eventually being able to close down at a moment's notice if faced with a sudden shock. Do choose an image which allows you to visualise opening and closing. Practise opening and closing each chakra in turn. A very good time to do this is just before you go to sleep, especially if you leave them closed for the night, because it can enable a better night's sleep.

### *Exercise 2 – Feeling the energies*

1 Creating frictional energy which is similar to the energy created by the particles' friction can easily be demonstrated by rubbing together your hands. This creates energy in the form of heat. Pull your hands away from each other slowly. Can you feel tension between them?

2 This second exercise is a stronger demonstration. Imagine that you have an opening in the palm of each hand. Now visualise a beam of white light energy coming from each palm. Do this for a few minutes and notice any sensations

you find building up. They are all pleasant so do not feel concerned. You may feel any or all of the following:

- a sense of heat
- a sense of tension, like a slack balloon between your hands, if you move them in and out slightly
- tingling in the fingers
- sensations running up and down your arms
- slight pins and needles
- a sense of excitement.

This is the energy field of our aura and it reflects different colours related to the emotional charges which we are emitting. These colours can be read by very advanced intuitives, or psychics, to identify health and emotional states and in some cases a whole emotional history. Past lives can also be read in this way.

### Exercise 3 – Starlight bubbles

Imagine you are sitting in a beautiful natural place. It can be a field or garden, or anywhere you feel most safe. Imagine that high up in the heavens there is a star and it is moving towards you at great speed, rushing down from the universe to protect you. As it comes closer, it slows and comes to a halt just over your head, about 12 inches above. Now it releases its energy as a beautiful white light which covers your whole body. It folds itself underneath your feet and moves with your limbs. See your arms and legs surrounded as you move them about in front of you. As you move around within this white light bubble you are completely protected and safe, you can see all that is happening around you, you can see the negative thoughts and emotions from others coming towards you but they just bend off the white light bubble and only the gentle words come through, as you allow them to. You are completely in control of what is allowed through this bubble.

### Exercise 4 – Feeling colours

Buy some very large coloured sheets of paper to meditate with. You may need to mount them or hang them on the wall. Sit close enough so that you cannot see anything else and really absorb the energy of the colour. Breathe in and fill your senses with each of 8 the colours in turn, spending at least 15–20 minutes on each colour. Notice what you are feeling, what physical sensations are occurring as you continue to do this exercise with each colour. It is a good idea to only do one colour each day as the different effects become confused and overlapping. Make a note of any ongoing effects in your energy levels over the next couple of days.

*Exploring states of consciousness enables us to explore our own minds more fully.*

# Altering Our States of Consciousness – 1

States of consciousness are different experiences, different levels of awareness and differing variations of brain waves. The next two chapters explore these experiences, including overviews of healing from relevant belief systems.

Commonly accepted altered states of consciousness include:

◆ dreams/daydreams

◆ hypnosis

◆ meditation

◆ trance journeys

◆ drug-induced states

◆ vicarious emotions (e.g. film, book, media influenced emotional states derived from other people).

As already discussed, altered states are useful for contacting different aspects of ourselves. Apart from the use of drugs, the important thing to know is that they all occur naturally. Many people will experience each of these states and remain unaware of it.

In some cultures hallucinogenic drugs are used to induce trance states but it is preferable to approach this kind of self-development without including anything that may have deleterious side-effects on the individual mind or body. Alcohol and caffeine both induce altered states of consciousness, alertness, loss of inhibitions and relaxation, or anxiety and tension/shaking and disorientation. Avoid vicarious emotions as much as possible. They create distractions to an awareness of your own real emotions about what is occurring in your own life right here and now.

## Establish your own base line of experience

An excellent exercise at this stage is to go on a diet of abstinence from external stimulants. I did this for three months and found the experience enlightening. It illustrates the difference between true feelings and feelings manipulated by things outside your immediate sphere of experience, e.g distressing or annoying items of news, events in soap operas.

For three months live without as much of the following as you can:

◆ coffee, tea or any form of caffeine
◆ alcohol, nicotine and other forms of drug
◆ all forms of media including films, newspapers
◆ fiction, leisure books and magazines
◆ gossip and interest in the minutiae of other people's lives (not real needs for/offers of support since this is part of your own experience)
◆ chemically produced and highly processed foods (if possible eat only vegetarian and organically grown food, whatever is comfortable for you).

Keep a record of the changes in your emotions and levels of awareness. You may be surprised at how different you start to feel. You will begin to know the meaning of true relaxation, rather than diversion from what you are feeling. This teaches you who you really are and what you really feel. As far as food is concerned, I include it here because if everything that exists is created by universal energy, and carries different vibrational frequencies, then food contains energy vibrations. Vibrations from distressed foodstuffs (slaughtered animals) may introduce negative energy directly into your body.

## Dreaming awareness

We are all aware of our dreams. Even if you do not regularly remember your dreams you have certainly experienced some which had an impact on you. All natural sleep includes REM sleep which is dreaming sleep. Only drug-induced sleep is dreamless. Dreaming is a natural experience which offers access into deeper levels of consciousness.

## Remembering dreams

Getting into the habit of remembering dreams can be difficult to begin with, but go to sleep with the full intention of remembering your dreams.

◆ Placing a pen and pad next to your bed emphasises this intention to the subconscious mind.

◆ Go to bed with a specific question on your mind and tell your subconscious mind to show you what is appropriate, then release the desire to your highest possible good.

◆ Set your alarm clock to ring approximately five or six hours into your sleep time to catch lighter sleep cycles when dreaming mostly occurs and record your experience.

Record dreams in your diary. Their meaning may appear random or obscure and take some time to become clear. If the dream is not recorded fully as soon as possible, it can become lost or distorted.

## Dreaming consciously

Dreams are still not fully understood as a result of any research that has been done through conventional psychology, although recent research into the experiences of lucid dreaming shows that a remarkable level of conscious control over the process is possible for some people. A lucid dream is when the individual is fully asleep yet fully aware that they are dreaming, to the point where they can influence their dream content and indicate this awareness to the researcher through an agreed signal. Some people become experienced in knowing when they are dreaming and being able to interpret their own imagery.

**Case Study: Lucid Dreaming and Recognising Metaphors – Kelly McK. Kelly's dream**

'I think you just know when a dream is important – intuitively. You remember every detail most vividly and know that you need to pay attention to it on waking – scribble it down, think about it or tell someone. In my dream I got out of bed and looked in the mirror. My hair was black (I see my hair as red now and black represented the me I've left behind – 16-ish gothic, trashy period – in other dreams I have seen a vision of me as a bright blonde, pale in a green cloak – she is the sensible one). I had woken up in an alternative reality. My parents were there sitting on an old sofa in the dingy room that had replaced the living room of my flat. My current boyfriend was there but he was an old boyfriend too. I sat next to him on the other sofa. He gave me fish and chips and the fish was raw and the chips were cold. It was horrid but I knew I had to go back there. I had a lot of jumpers on, one from my stepfather, one of my mother's, one a gothically tatty one, one of my ex-boyfriend's and a sporty one. I took them all off and picked up my pillow (from the bed where I slept, it had been in their dingy room) then I said goodbye and left the house. I walked down the road. It was like New York or somewhere big and loud and alive. I noticed that no other single women were walking about. I passed a diner, through the window I could see all the booths were packed. I thought of going in for a bit of safety but knew it was false security so I passed by. I continued down the road under a canopied area. A man with a tray of small milk portions and a large straw was trying to give them to me but I knew you couldn't drink like that, that it was a trick. He had me cornered so I willed myself to fly up to the canopy and punched through it. I flew through a beautiful, stormy sky and dropped back onto my bed here in my bedroom (at this point the scene was totally naturalistic again).

'I went to the mirror to check my hair colour ( which signalled which reality I was in). It was red now. I saw that it was 10.11 a.m. by the green clock on the desk in my bedroom, but the room was dim and when I looked outside it was dark. That's when I realised I had not really woken up – as it would be light at that time. It was rainy, almost dark, and too cloudy to see more than a foot in front of you. I went into the living room, and the furniture and possessions had all been piled into the middle as if someone had broken in. I was wearing what I was actually wearing in bed, pyjama bottoms and a vest top. The neighbours came in. They had been 'burgled' too. I showed them into my flat and I noticed that there was a dusty old stereo unit. All the tapes had been pulled out of the casings and it had been destroyed. The neighbours and I went outside and my boyfriend, a work mate and my brother joined us. We walked until the house (mine) was in front of us but it was down a country lane on an unmade road, all on its own. The sun was shining and it was really lovely. We passed a yard and I saw a man lying on the floor surrounded by chickens. We recognised each other immediately and I knew that he was very wise. Then he changed to being a puppy and the others were grown dogs. I said to the puppy a few times, 'we need your help' making gestures as if doing sign language, touching the heart, the lips then reaching out to him. The puppy couldn't understand as easily as the man, but there was a spark of it still and he got up and followed us. The chicken/dog things followed him. As we all continued up the farm track to our house, I wondered what a puppy was going to do against the forces that smashed up our flats, but I trusted it because I had recognised the face of an ancient teacher before he had metamorphosed. We arrived and I went into my room and woke up for real.'

### Kelly's own interpretations

'I did actually will myself to do things, travel and fly and make decisions, within the dream. I was controlling my responses as things happened to me and choosing how things would work out in the end. When I smashed through the ceiling I was worried that there would be more underneath and I would be trapped but I willed there to be just the stormy sky.

'The metaphor in the dream told me:

'In the other reality, the dingy room, I saw my amber cross on a wooden panel on a hook. The bottom had snapped off. I tried to explain to the boyfriend character that in the other reality it wasn't broken. Belief in many possible realities. Not being understood/able to be listened to properly by others. When I was 7-ish I played with a black mongrel puppy at night. Imaginary friend but I did actually see him. Hair colours symbolic of stages of life development – images of self in fashion styles. Layers of clothes stripping away layers of images adopted, all not me. Approached by scary man – common theme – overcome imaginary fears – want to be rescued hide in booth – know that is not any good and I will overcome it myself. Calling for help.'

Some time after the dream Kelly separated from the 'current boyfriend' of the dream.

This dream is rich in imagery and metaphor. There is much more in it which will begin to make sense to Kelly as things occur in her life. For now she has all the understanding she needs to work with. We often take some time to be able to understand the contents of dreams but several themes come up regularly for Kelly, especially being misunderstood, not being listened to and being scared of calling for help. By using her dreams she was able to recognise deep unconscious fears and confront them as being of no power or influence in her life.

When recording dreams you gradually develop an understanding of the metaphors which your unconscious mind uses.

## Dreaming for inspiration

Dreams are a very good and reliable source of intuitive inspiration. Although this may not seem clear initially, they contain layers of meaning which become apparent when something is recognised from the outside world. If we do not record dreams fully as they are remembered they may not be repeated and the insight is lost. They tell us things about ourselves of which we are unaware.

**Case Study: Dreams Showing Talents and Directions**_____

Jane woke one morning having had a most peculiar dream which she could not understand. It seemed quite bizarre. It was so clear and precise, she was sure it had meaning and wrote it down. 'I was sitting in my kitchen when just outside the doorway into the hall six bright lights appeared, like small flying points of light, about 2 cms in diameter. They were dancing about and I felt unsure of them. I turned my attention to one of them and willed it to leave. It vanished. I turned my attention to another but it dissolved through the wall and into the outside. Another two followed it. Then one turned and fired two beams of light straight into my eyes before leaving quite slowly, with the final one close behind it. It felt as if they had switched something in the back of my brain, like a door opening.

'Suddenly I could see things that were happening a long way off. It was fun. I could see all sorts of things, past and future too. Then I tried to use it to see into the life of someone I knew and the vision was lost. That was when I awoke.'

The dream was clearly an indication of an ability which was already within Jane but which she had to learn to use with correct judgement. It demonstrated her considerable clairvoyancy ability but also to use these powers with respect, especially for others. As soon as she misused them, to spy, they were taken from her._____

## Interpreting dreams

Dreams help us to interpret something that has already happened. This is retrospective dreaming, often showing a new dimension which we may or may not understand. It is an opportunity to learn from mistakes, like Jane above. If we record dreams we can then see which are retrospective and which are predictive.

When you keep a dream diary you begin to realise you have

been deleting the time aspect of it, or flipping it over because it is not generally acceptable to believe that one is dreaming before the event, and we tend to remember the event as if it happened before the dream. A very high proportion of dreams are the other way around, they are precognitive but of incredibly boring details. However, self-knowledge includes the mundane and the exciting.

## Sleeping to dream

Sleep on your right side, allowing your left nostril to open and connect with your right brain throughout the night. This can create a deeper response to dream messages. Give it several nights and record all experiences. Some people have difficulty remembering dreams, but if it is a lucid dream you will. Asking a question before you go to bed, to be shown something relevant for a situation you face, can be enough to stimulate dreams.

## Meeting regular characters

Sometimes dreams feature specific, regular characters. These characters can become realities during our daytimes too. One interpretation is that they are guides. Children remember these experiences more than most, although guides can also be contacted through all forms of altered consciousness except vicarious emotions. The range of experiences is enormous but two common themes emerge:

- ◆ we are taken on fantastic journeys, can fly and have all sorts of adventures
- ◆ we are protected and tutored in skills or beliefs.

## Working with guides

The most important aspect of developing intuition is learning to trust how and what it tells us. A commonly used aspect of intuition is to work with guides with whom we develop a special relationship of trust. This works well for many people. A guide may be a Jungian archetype, a metaphorical figure representing some aspect of your unconscious mind, or they may really exist. The arguments are so subjective you must decide yourself what you believe or accept. Work with your own beliefs, whatever they are now, and let your own experiences guide you into extending these further if appropriate.

## Trusting the guides

For people who work with guides, they are completely real and unquestionable. For those who do not, they are just another way of repressing your higher unconscious mind, or using a metaphor to represent higher truth and power.

**Case Study: Angels as Friends**_____

Brittnay was 3 years old when she first mentioned to her parents the name Tonya. She would scream in the middle of the night, but when her parents went in to her she would be sleeping. One morning her parents asked her who Tonya was and she said, 'Tonya is an angel who climbs in my window at night and takes me up to heaven to be an angel.' Brittnay has said that Tonya is specifically her angel and when asked how she got to be an angel was told, 'she died and there was blood all over . . . Tonya was killed and broke her leg. Tonya was 4 years old.'

About six months later a child of friends died and Brittnay went with her mother to put flowers on the grave. Brittnay told her mother, 'I lived here at the cemetery and also Tonya did,' and she pointed to a part of the cemetery. The mother has not yet verified the gravestones and this is too far away (North America) for me to verify. But it is an interesting case study, typical of childhood psychic guide experiences. The family had never taught Brittnay about angels and are often asked if they can see her too. Brittnay has since been diagnosed with two medical conditions – Perthes disease, which is to do with the blood supply to the hip, and epilepsy. She is now 7 and still sees Tonya regularly. At first it was almost nightly but now several times per month. Brittnay has become very curious about religious ideas and clearly finds a great deal of comfort from her relationship with Tonya. Possibly the grave is there and identifiable, but the most important point of this story is the length of time this guide has been with Brittnay, over four years, through some rough times, and how comfortable and real Tonya is to Brittnay. There is a follow-up to Brittnay's story. Shortly after the graveyard event, Brittnay's mother, Andra, was deep in thought about these experiences whilst driving, to the extent that she missed a green traffic light. As she looked up, she saw another driver coming across her path, jumping the red light. If she had noticed the green light she would have been involved in a very nasty accident. Was the angel in Andra's mind to protect her too? I do not believe in coincidence. I believe it could have been a guide or some deeper aspect of Andra's unconscious, intuitively keeping her focused elsewhere._____

Several types of guide are recognised. They can be living humans we meet and know or a spirit form. My own childhood guide for many years was a wonderful native American healer who taught me to cope with fear through my dreams and to challenge my fear of darkness, to know I was always safe. He worked a lot through my dreams. Just before I went to bed he would arrive and support me conquering my fear of darkness and night. Now I love the mysteries and energies of night. He left me at the onset of puberty. I missed him, but met up with him again recently when he joined me for this part of my life. I am aware of him at times but rarely communicate as clearly as I did in childhood. I feel his messages sometimes, they are mostly about knowing what is real and what is not, about truths and illusion. He is a master guide.

## Different guides

You may work with one guide or many. Some kinds of guide are identified below:

1  Angels, the first guides we receive at the time of birth and who see you safely through your life so that you complete the goal and lessons to be learned for this life. Angels protect us from spiritual and physical danger unless it is part of our chosen path to experience.

2  Service guides, also called runners or helpers. Runners help you find and notice things, directing your attention appropriately, e.g. recognising synchronistic experiences. Helpers work with specific problems and intervene at your request.

3  Teachers, these help you to remember who you are when you are feeling low, to seek the help that you need at the right time in your life. Reading this book may be the result of a teacher guiding you to it. Teachers bring understanding

through those around you and your experiences, they are the metaphorical light bulb when we understand something properly for the first time.

4   Masters, very caring guides who are totally devoted to overseeing your life journey as you move from one level of knowing to another. The growth of spiritual awareness is closely linked to intuition and your master leads you towards the inspiration you need when you need it most. It is a healing guide who brings enlightenment, helps us release the past and become fully healed from all the anger, hurt and fear we have held on to for our whole life.

5   Joy guides are the guides which help us have fun, make us feel the inner child spirit, wanting to run through piles of dried leaves or splash in the sea. The guides want us to enjoy the moment fully and recognise the reality that negative experience is what we create for ourselves through our own perceptions.

**Case Study: Judy's Guides**_____

Judy had lost her house and car keys; the complete bunch had just disappeared. She could not remember where it was. she went to bed concerned that her home might not be secure, nor her car, but asked her guides to lead her to whatever the purpose of this unexpected loss was, and let it go so that her sleep would not be disturbed. She trusted and because she was a very organised person who rarely lost anything, believed that the keys would turn up when it was appropriate. The following morning Judy checked around the house again and then had to phone someone who had a set of her house keys and go and collect them. This was someone who had been staying and had left with bad feeling. Judy had been reluctant to request the keys' return but now had little choice. She explained what had happened. She had the keys returned to her immediately on request and returned home. Within ten minutes of arriving back at her house she saw her own set of keys lying in a quite obvious place. She thanked her guides, angels, helpers and runners, who had combined forces to lead her through this experience, whatever it might have been; she would never know exactly.

## *Using guides*

Guides are apparently there helping us in spite of ourselves, but if we open up to them and ask for their help they will be even more available to us. If using a guide is a useful metaphor for asking our higher self to guide us through a situation, then this is as good an explanation as any. The 'proof' is in the use and the success it brings.

We trust that when we flick a light switch it will work, we do not worry that it may be in a mood with us and decide not to work for us. If it does not work we do not take it personally. This is how to work with guides. They will help you but only for your highest personal good. That is their only agenda and so you will get what you ask for, whatever that need is, because it will contain learning. If you ask for something that is selfish and greedy or unkind to others, you will get that and the consequences of that request will also be yours, to teach you to think about what you want and why. If you ask for things in love then you will receive them in love.

## Recognising false guides and fear

The biggest false guide we have is our ego. This has been turned into two acronyms which are equally appropriate:

◆ Earth Guide Only
◆ or Easing God Out.

The ego wants to stay in control and this is the voice which will try to convince you that everything in this book is a load of nonsense. Typical ego arguments are:

◆ you'll look a fool if you believe this
◆ where's the real proof, the scientific evidence
◆ this is just wishful thinking
◆ who are your trying to con, because you won't get me
◆ if I can't see it then it can't be true.

Ego likes to take the credit for itself and can become inflated at times. But anything that can become elevated and make us feel better can also be deflated and make us feel down. It is a vulnerable and false guide. A quiet sense of knowing oneself, and being open to each experience as coming from deeper within ourselves and connecting to a universal force, leaves us much less vulnerable to the whimsical nature of every-day ups and downs. If we accept that our successes and our failures are of *equal* importance to our overall progress and learning, then we can flow tranquilly through life and contemplate that nothing is negative. It is very fear-releasing. 'Failures' are mastering new dimensions of ourselves.

## Developing ego

Developmental psychology states that ego development is an essential stage in consciousness of a child, and the recognition that they are separate from other people. Freud identifies the ego as developing within a few months of birth. He states its role as being the executive, making decisions and problem-solving, the logical reasoning processes. It is very much a left brain aspect. It is the conflict between the ego, the more basic urges of the id, and the conscience/guilt voices of the superego, that creates differences in personality.

Young children are born with a sense of connectedness which they lose to varying degrees according to their childhood experiences and levels of self-awareness.

> Developing intuition is reconnecting with that sense of oneness through understanding and experience.

Our society teaches us to be separated from each other. Human experience is based on isolation and individuation, and through this we recognise our responsibility for our own life and development. We are born from oneness and we become individual so that we can return to oneness consciously. Remaining separated from the oneness of the universe and self is a state of fear and isolation that is damaging to the spirit. It is the basis of emotional breakdowns, depression and other mental illnesses. Through developing our intuition we get a strong feeling of connectedness to our higher selves and the greater sense of living. Through connecting with our true selves, we never feel alone and the thoughts, feelings and attitudes of those around us do not adversely affect us.

## Experiencing shamanic dream times

Most shamanic teaching comes from native peoples of the Americas. They have a very spiritual tradition based in the ideas of oneness/harmony with the environment and with the self. For these teachings the oneness is called Great Mystery, and is understood to be the original source of all. Dreaming and altered states of consciousness feature highly in these traditions. Dreamtime is seen as a special and sacred experience of connecting with oneself There are two ways of using dreams: the obvious sleeptime dreams outlined below, and out of body dreamtimes which are explored in the next chapter. These latter connect to ideas of alternative realities or parallel universes. In these traditions, sleeptime dream interpretations vary slightly but generally are divided into categories of dreams which form a kind of hierarchy of importance.

1 **No secret dreams** are dreams which are too vague to leave you with anything much to work with. These are of least significance.

2 **Abundance dreams** contain information about property and wealth, however that may be manifested in your life. Sometimes they will tell what you must do to allow abundance into your life, other times they will show you what to expect.

3 **Wish dreams** assist in identifying your hopes and dreams for the future. These dreams can only come true if there is sufficient trust that they will and no conflicting beliefs.

4 **Healing dreams** or **medicine dreams** are bringers of the future with clarity. These dreams are a rare and special gift. They should not be ignored and should only be shared with great respect and caution.

## Summary

Since you are already going through many different states of consciousness on a daily basis, getting to know and recognise them is the most obvious next step.

♦ Dreams are potentially great sources of healing and teaching, this is recognised in many different cultural traditions.

- ◆ Dreams offer opportunities to explore yourself more deeply and become acquainted with your own metaphorical interpretations of experience.
- ◆ Dreams are a natural part of human experience and are experienced by everyone.
- ◆ Training yourself to remember and work with dreams is quite simple once the intention is there.

CHAPTER 12

# Altering Our States of Consciousness – 2

T his chapter continues exploring states of mind using methods which are self-induced and voluntary, whereas dreaming may not be. These states of mind are entered intentionally, to develop greater familiarity with your own inner workings.

It is generally accepted that human understanding of the brain is minimal compared to the apparent potential. These types of experiences are part of that potential, and suggest far greater levels of awareness than we can begin to imagine at present. By exploring these ideas, you will find yourself opening to those possibilities.

### Breathing yourself calm

Most altered states of consciousness require that you are relaxed and calm. Breathing is one of the most profound ways of doing that. The following styles of breathing are worth experimenting with.

1   Breathing from the diaphragm, place your hand over your stomach, just below your ribcage, and feel your hand moving out/up as your breathe in and down/in as you breathe out. Breathe slowly as you count a rhythm for each complete breath. Continue this for about 4–5 minutes, noticing how you feel.

2   As above but consciously choose to relax more deeply on each out-breath until you are very relaxed.

3   Breathe in counted cycles, breathing in to the count of 3 or 4, hold it for the same count, breathe out for the same count, and hold it for the same count. Continue this for a few minutes, noticing how clear your mind becomes.

4    Breathe naturally from the diaphragm and notice the
      sensation of the breath entering and leaving your nostril.
      Focus completely on this sensation and continue breathing.
      Come back to the sensation as soon as you find your
      concentration wandering.

## Preparing for altered states of consciousness

With all the following techniques it is a good idea to ensure
the following precautions for your own comfort.

- Work in a place where you feel warm and comfortable.
- Make sure you will not be disturbed or interrupted for your
  allocated duration.
- Give yourself space to sit comfortably or lie down.
- Take phones off the hook and switch off doorbells etc if
  possible.
- Burning incense sticks and white candles leaves an
  atmosphere cleared of residual negative energies.
- Always begin by breathing rhythmically, as in one of the
  previous exercises, or just in your own preferred way. Take
  time to become completely relaxed.
- The more you 'try' to enter one of these states the more
  you will be unable – using conscious mind or will. Trying
  is not letting go and allowing things to happen.
  If you are concerned about coming back on time, set a
  gentle alarm which will alert you to the need to return at a
  specific time, or set a tape with a wake up call on a timer
  switch. This enables you to relax more fully.

## Experiencing hypnosis

There is much misunderstanding surrounding hypnosis, largely
due to the popularity of stage hypnosis. Most clinical
hypnotherapists professionally disassociate themselves from
stage hypnosis. Hypnosis is a state of letting go and allowing
things to happen, *but* you are not out of control at all. In fact
you are very much in control all the time. There are two
fundamental points to this misconception.

- Hypnosis works on our belief systems, so if you believe that
  a hypnotist has power over you, they do because you have
  allowed this.

◆ If you know that this cannot be the case, there is nothing to fear.

Many tapes available allow you to take yourself into hypnosis and out again. It is simply a skill which can be learned and developed to suit your needs for relaxation. Many people are surprised at how easy and how pleasant it is.

Hypnosis is a deeply relaxed state of consciousness, ideal for facilitating guided visualisation journeys using the powers of imagination. Although it is deeply relaxing and allows us to let go, which is therapeutic to some degree, hypnosis is most effective as a tool combined with other techniques. One aim is to take your imagination on a guided journey to meet someone like a guide or to find an answer to something that has been troubling you. These are basically higher self, or unconscious images which help us gain insight into specifics and release redundant aspects of ourselves, especially limitation beliefs.

## Doing visualisations

It is a good idea to transfer the words of a printed visualisation onto tape, and listen to it through headphones, having completed a relaxation exercise beforehand. Using imagination automatically accesses the right brain and unconscious mind, which enables us to drift effortlessly into a hypnotic state. Alternatively, find someone you are comfortable with to read this journey to you and just allow yourself to follow the words in your imagination.

Some people have difficulty 'seeing' images. This is fine. You are not getting it wrong if you do not 'see' because in the intuitive sense see means a general experience, an impression, a feeling that you can know something without having empirical evidence.

### The Magic Pool of Wisdom – a visualisation journey

This script should be read at a leisurely pace, with pauses indicated by dots, and last approximately 8–10 minutes.
*Imagine that you are walking along a path which is meandering through the countryside, through a field of beautiful wild*

*flowers... It is a warm summer's day... There is a gentle breeze which makes the flowers sway gently and wafts their scent towards you... Butterflies dance across the surface of the field... The breeze refreshes you as you are walking... and you can feel the grass softly under your feet.*

*At the edge of the field there are trees... The path is leading you towards the edge of a forest... As you enter the trees, see how the sunlight filters down through the leaves, leaving small patches of sunlight on the floor of the forest. The path leads you further into the forest... You can feel the cool refreshing shade of the trees... the silence and tranquillity of the forest... The trees are old and majestic... The floor of the forest is carpeted with old leaves and moss... and here and there small clumps of flowers growing in the patches of sunlight. The path is easy to follow and begins to wind around a clump of bushes, towards a clearing in the centre of the forest... In the centre of the clearing a small pool of clear water sparkles in the sunlight. The banks are grassy... soft ... and inviting to sit on... Find a place where you would like to sit and make yourself comfortable...*

*This pool is a magic pool. Its water is healing and holds gifts of insight and wisdom. You have come here with a question to ask of the pool and to offer it a gift. The pool has magic qualities and is able to take a burden from you, something which is troubling you, holding you back from finding your purpose in life. It may be guilt, or fear, or self doubt... Whatever it is the pool will take it from you and cleanse you. Put your hands into the water now... Feel the refreshing coolness and stillness of the pool... Feel the water drawing from you all the negative feelings and thoughts which you have, self doubt, anger... Whatever they are, feel the water taking these negative feelings and transforming them into wisdom and knowledge... healing them all. Feel the water, as pure love, flowing and swirling around your hands as you move them around in the water...*

*As you continue to do this you feel yourself becoming more and more relaxed... calm... More confident... A quiet knowingness forms... A knowledge and wisdom of all that you have been and experienced... that has led you to this point in your life... to this place by the pool... Now take your hands from the water and wait until the surface is smooth again... Keep watching the water See how smooth and clear it is... Now a slight image is beginning to appear in the pool. It is quite small at first and seems to be coming from deep below... The outline is getting bigger... and swirling patterns form on the surface of the water... Now you can see it quite closely... it is an image which the pool has made from all that you released into its water... it is a message for you, an insight into your higher purpose, your future. It answers your question... and it changes and moves, showing you images which take you further into your true self, your true purpose...*

*Now the images start to fade... and the surface of the water sparkles again in the sunlight... You can leave the pool now... and follow the path back through the forest... back through the field and the wild flowers in the sunshine... Now... in your own time... come back to the room bringing with you all the insight and understanding that you have gained.*

Often the imagery and meaning from these journeys is immediately apparent, but occasionally we do not fully understand all we are told. Write down all you remember because even small details mean something and deeper levels of meaning become apparent at a later date, as our understanding increases.

## Taking trance journeys

This kind of journeying comes from shamanic traditions and is different from guided visualisation. Instead of imagination following a script, it is an out of body experience and you wait to see what is shown to you when you arrive at your destination. Shamanic journeying is rooted in a belief system.

### *Shamanic belief systems*

Shamanism believes in seven levels of evolution of the spirit and many reincarnations. Humans are at fourth-mind level, currently moving towards fifth level. These levels mirror the development of the embryo through to and beyond adulthood, the chakras and recent scientific discoveries.

## Level one

The first level is mineral, a holding level, and relates to the base chakra, our connection to mother earth. Mother earth is seen as a beautiful goddess, impregnated by her spiritual husband. All life forms on earth are offspring of this union. It is related to the idea that the planet started off with a mineral soup from which life evolved. We all spent some time living as mineral life forms. This is the level of the fertilised ovum. If one of her offspring (humans) threatens the survival of others, she will cause great disturbance to cleanse the harm and heal the life (natural disasters). We have a natural affinity to minerals and need them in our body structure. We are drawn to them and value them highly as ornament for our bodies. Most people will pick up stones without wondering why, and children have favourite stones they collect.

## Level two

This is plant level, the second stage of evolution, also our use of plants as food. This level is connected to our physical bodies, to the second chakra, our reproductive and creative functions. It relates to the growth of the embryo into a small human form. It is our body to treat as we choose or abuse. It relates to physical fitness and indicates we should be more careful with what we take into our bodies: good food, natural healthy exercise, communion with the natural plant world around us, our affinity with plants and flowers, our need to see greenery for relaxation and tranquillity. It relates to all the automatic functions of our bodies and those of which we are unaware, like our hearts pumping blood and oxygen around our bodies all the time without our thinking about it or doing anything to make it happen. It concerns the size and shape of our bodies, why we have this particular body, the lessons it teaches us.

## Level three

This is animal level, referred to as the child self or hidden self. This is the level of learned or automatic responses. It is below thinking level and is our instinctive base. Often overridden by our conscious mind, it is the centre of our emotional bodies and can have a devastating effect on our bodies and lives if not worked with consciously. At this level love is not emotion but a vibrational frequency to which we can tune ourselves. It is the highest and most perfect frequency to tune into. We experience this through our love links with other people, but it can be an unbalanced and painful experience if the other levels in our body are not balanced. It is the state to aim for, to radiate love to all those around us. But we have to listen to the child inside us, and work sensitively to heal that part of self. When we do not, we experience fear and the uncontrolled tyranny of emotions become very destructive. We feel lost and alone, separated from the oneness of the universe. Unbalance and disconnectedness is the basis for all mental and physical illness in spiritual terms.

## The fourth level

The level of human mind, the one we are most familiar with. It is mental energy, the power of logical thought. It relates to the fourth chakra, our compassion and knowledge of all around us. We have our awareness centred in our minds most of the time. It relates to adulthood, conscious of all around us through empathy and intuition. It is to do with perception; that we interpret the world which we think we see in our own way, but our perception is limited because there are many things relating to the higher levels to which we have not yet travelled. This level is uniquely human. We must remember that we do not all perceive things in the same way, or as other animals on the planet. We all have our own levels of understanding which should be respected to the highest level, as being all part of the offspring of mother earth.

## Shamanic healing principles

It is essential to heal the levels up to this point in order to reach contact with the higher levels, or we risk unbalance and distress. We are only trapped by our human awareness if we do not heal these levels and move beyond them by choice. By experiencing a harmonious existence up to this level we will automatically find ourselves opening to higher levels of perceptual awareness. We are only trapped by our human minds if we choose not to see that there is more beyond.

## The fifth level

The awareness to which we are aspiring and which relates to the fifth/communication chakra. This is soul level, the realm of higher self. We visit this level in dreams and trance journeys. This is the part that is the sum of all that we are and have ever been during previous lives on earth. This is our communication of thought energies which create material manifestations of our inner reality and is a very powerful energy force in the universe. This is the ray of energy which is *you*, passing through the universe and being part of it. You are an aspect of your soul, it is not an aspect of you, and reminding ourselves of this regularly allows us to relate to that higher self more easily. You may experience this level as flashes of inspiration and understanding as your higher self guides you through your lessons and touches your human mind. It also relates to experiences of floating above yourself, leaving your body, astral travel and near death experiences.

## Levels six and seven

These relate to the source of all, of which we are a part. The physical manifestation of this is the sun on which all life depends. Words are a fourth level tool and woefully inadequate to express these higher levels. We must experience them rather than know it as an explanation. (Zen Buddhism suggests that if you can explain then it is not true Zen.) Level seven is a higher source even than the sun. It is the level of god in all of us, a state of pure being which has no physical manifestation to relate to. We can think of ourselves as points of pure energy or light. As each point or light ray becomes separate from the others it condenses and becomes mental energy, and so on down to the lower levels.

## Connecting everything

The shamanic web which connects all levels, and of which we

are a part, means that all levels are also connected and are not separate from each other. So we are able to reach all levels but from aspects of ourselves which contain those higher levels, not from the human mind level. When we sleep we are experiencing levels six and seven but are unable to interpret this in fourth level mind. This ancient belief system clearly reflects recent scientific developments in understanding the nature of existence.

## Shamanic journeying

This is voluntary entering of the parallel realities. The parallel dreamtime reality is where your spirit self resides, from where it is continuously sending messages and guidance. It can appear completely identical but information missed in human reality is noted and fed back to you from this alternative reality. It is journeying into the past (Lower World) or future (Upper World), and holds many parallels with modern techniques of regression for healing. It is intended to put you in touch with your inner child or animal self.

This is generally taught with the guidance of a shamanic teacher's support but it is possible to develop this ability in yourself. Some have this ability naturally.

## Taking a journey

Lying down, cover yourself with a blanket so that your body cannot become tense with cold. If you are relaxed your awareness can leave your body more easily. Allow yourself to relax fully through breathing exercises. You will find a drumming tape most useful for this experience (addresses at back of book). Drumming sets up the vibrations which ease you out of this reality.

1   Relax and prepare yourself. Visualise yourself in a place where you feel very comfortable and safe. It can be somewhere you are familiar with or an imaginary place.
2   Visualise yourself near a pool or close to a cave, rabbit hole or some other opening which you can travel down. Think of Alice and the white rabbit in *Alice in Wonderland* or the story of Persephone entering the realms of Hades, from Greek mythology.

3   As you relax and work with your images, use the intention of going down this opening into the Lower World.

4   Begin to travel down this passageway, feel yourself moving down through realities to this other place. You find your normal senses are not functioning in the usual way because you are moving beyond their realms. You are sensing things and are able to see or feel in differing ways.

5   Take a good look around and see where you are. Make a note of all that you experience and stay as long as you feel comfortable. To begin with it's a good idea just to visit and look around, then return to human reality. Once you have journeyed a few times you can begin to stay for longer periods and explore further.

6   Return from the same direction you entered, back through the tunnel. This can seem much quicker and easier than the journey down.

The important thing to remember is that you are not experiencing anything that is not already within you, but you may not have been aware of it before. It is not the same thing as visualisation, which is fourth level mind. You may have to practise this technique a few times before you achieve a full journey so do not give up after your first attempt.

## Paganism

Paganism is a belief system which is matriarchal in its references. The principal belief is in the three aspects of female:

◆   the maid
◆   the mother
◆   the wise old woman, sometimes called the hag.

Both shamanism and paganism are labelled 'occult'.

Occult simply means unseen, so things which are hidden from easy sight are called the occult. Although many religions have interpreted the realms of the dark goddess as evil, this is their fear response to things which they cannot control. Hence the murder of psychics and wisewomen as witches and children of the devil. They communed with the hidden side of living, as we all do anyway, but so often we hide from the conscious relationship with the dark side.

Life is divided into cycles: winter–summer, night–day, birth–death and so on. The dark goddess is in charge of the death, winter and night part of life, the bright goddess is the day, summer aspect. Each is equally needed for the other to exist. This is like yin and yang.

## The dark goddess

The dark goddess appears in many belief systems, including Christianity, and is called many names: Kali, Tara, Isis, the Sheikinah, Anu, Mari, Margaine, Persephone, Hecate, Morrighan, Rhiannon, Lilith, Black Madonna, Mary Magdalene, the last two being from the heretical Christian systems such as Cathars.

Paganism sees life as one big matrix, which is linked to moon stages, including sexuality and powers of creativity and procreation. Thus these characters were seen as evil because of their great passions and contact with the intuitive nature of humankind. It is not a matriarchy in the way that we live in a patriarchy where male influence has so much of the power and would seek to take it away from women. It treats male and female as equal with different roles in the matrix of life.

Many paradoxes exist, such as how can the dark goddess, who is goddess of the other world, also be so involved in sexual passion and conception, which is the domain of the bright goddess in the daylight and the full moon? The paradox has great power, a mystery, because we cannot reduce it to a simple construct. It is like the concept of god or oneness – all is connected, all moves in cycles. She is often seen as a mourner at the graveside and sometimes this is seen as sinister. Yet we cannot have rebirth unless we have death. The problem in our society is that we try to separate everything in order to understand, rather than to understand it in its oneness. The concept of oneness occurs because they are all seen as part of the same matrix but with different aspects which complement each other. The dark goddess represents the inner realms of consciousness, inner journeys and development of intuitive power, healing powers of the mind.

It is possible to visit the realms of the dark goddess, the

space between lives, the dark moon of existence. She is often depicted across or near water and we may cross water to travel to the other side. Many meditations and rituals include water as a medium of healing, cleansing and baptism, as in the Magic Pool visualisation.

## Regressing into past lives

Journeys into our past lives can be achieved through hypnosis or journeys similar to the shamanic ones of going down long tunnels into the past, usually a tunnel with many doors, each of which represents a different life. Once you are relaxed and confident with these kind of experiences you may be able to take such journeys easily. They can occur spontaneously, on meeting up with a soul or spirit you recognise from a past life who has reincarnated here with you to meet up again in this life. This instant or spontaneous recall will often take a couple of days to fully clear but is a result of reading the energies from the other person's aura. Often the recall will serve to illustrate a parallel with an experience in this life, a part of the learning from previous lives which is being continued in this life.

**Case Study: Kelly C.**

I decided to have a bath as I'd had a busy day and wanted a nice long soak. Once I was in I thought I'd do some self-hypnosis to relax me even more. I looked at my watch and decided that 25 minutes was enough so told myself that I had to come back at half-past seven.

I started off as I always did, taking a few deep breaths, I closed my eyes and walked down the steps into my special garden where I sat on my bench under a weeping willow. As I sat down I didn't really know what I was going to think about, so I relaxed, felt the sun beating down on me and looked into the clouds to see if anything would come to me from the shapes of them. I was sitting looking at them for a few minutes, not seeing anything but relaxing even more. Suddenly without any warning I felt myself zooming up towards the clouds. At first I wasn't sure what was happening, I was going very fast and felt I was on a roller coaster but going up instead of down. All of a sudden I stopped, was lying down in mid-air and it was all very calm. I felt like a magician's assistant when they raise them from the table, as I was lying down with my now long hair hanging down (I have short hair). I looked down and could see myself still sitting on the bench in the garden.

I lay there for a few minutes and then stood up and started walking, not sure where I was going. Then I found myself in a large room, I looked round and thought I was on a set from Cleopatra, this is what it reminded me of. I looked around and figured I was in some sort of bathing dressing room and there were women in something like a Roman bath, fussing over each other. There were many large columns in the room and a stone floor. I was wearing strappy leather sandals, a long white dress with a thin gold cord around the waist and fastened on my left shoulder with a huge gold brooch. I remember thinking 'how beautiful', feeling it was very special to me. It had different coloured stones set in it and really was gorgeous. I then got a flash of myself from behind, my long hair was on top of my head with something entwined in it. It looked stunning. I walked out of the bathing room and found myself in another room with lots of people on red velvet couches. There were tables with gold bowls full of fruit and large gold wine goblets. Everybody was chatting to each other and they were all dressed like me. I went and sat down on one of the couches next to a man. He smiled, kissed my cheek and started chatting to me. I couldn't hear what he was saying. He had dark, tight curly hair but I couldn't make out his face, so I looked into his eyes. This was the strangest thing to happen so far. His eyes lit up and they were all I could see, they seemed to come out of his face. Then I recognised my brother's eyes. It happened in a split second but they were definitely Glenn's eyes.

We both stood up. He was dressed like me but his brooch didn't have stones set in it and his toga was short. We walked out of the room and I found myself in front of hundreds of people. We were standing at the top of some steps in front of a large building. The steps went round in a semi-circle and there were people everywhere. The man took hold of my hand and said to the crowd, 'I would like to present my new wife.' Everyone cheered. I don't know why but I felt very happy. We walked back inside and I got this feeling that I had to go. I turned to the man and told him that I would be back soon and I walked back to the bathing room. I walked through there and found myself back where I started, so I lay down and with that I went zooming down and found myself back on my bench in my garden. I stood up and walked back up the steps. I opened my eyes and there I was back in my bath at home. I looked at my watch and I had been just five minutes longer than I'd told myself to be.'

### Kelly's interpretation of her experience

This experience tells of the closeness between Kelly and her brother and suggests they had been close before and there is a special supportive relationship in this life. 'Glenn has always been there for me and talked to me, a very close friend as well as a brother.' Often there is nothing special in a past life recall other than to illustrate how different relationships offer different roles and teaching in our present lives with special people with whom we choose to incarnate._____

## Summary

With all these techniques, keeping an open mind leads you into some exciting experiences and gives you very different views on your present human reality. It all helps you to learn more about who you really are and what you are capable of at deeper levels.

- ◆ Never assume that what you know is all there is to know.
- ◆ Recognise that human experience is of itself limited and limiting but our minds can go far beyond the physical realms if we let them.
- ◆ Different belief systems offer us a rich range of different ways to understand human experience.
- ◆ Metaphor allows a clearer understanding of the reality by illustrating key points.

# Postscript – Finding the Web

I started to write this piece before the book was completed and knew it would be important but was not sure in which way. As I neared completion it became clear where I should use it. This book is about connections, with self, between different belief systems and ideas, with all that exists.

One sunny late September morning, I was visiting various websites on the internet to collect information and contacts for this book. I am still learning how to make best use of the web and all its intricacies. In spite of the extremely good tuition of my 15-year-old son for whom all this is like taking a walk in the park, I still find it hard to adapt to such a new system of communication when I have been used to standing in front of people talking, and of course listening, for a whole day teaching. Now I spend many days reading and writing.

I needed a break and my head was crying out for a walk in the garden. Feeling a tinge of guilt, I thankfully emptied the wet laundry from the machine. (I do still have the odd twinge of guilt about the most irrational things and I remind myself guilt is a pointless, negative emotional response since I take full responsibility for all my behaviour. It isn't easy living by your own rules.)

As I walked down to the washing line, my face was assaulted by many fine silver strands. The original and alternative 'web'. I considered how effective they were at catching victims for the spider to eat. What can be more beautiful than the sight of a spider's web glistening in the autumn sunshine with the droplets of dew still clinging to its fine silk strands?

It was walking through these webs that set the theme for my thoughts. The webs were hanging across the garden path, connecting plants from one side to another in a net that would catch unsuspecting flies with their tensile strength. I also considered the industry of each spider which I casually destroy in this walk down the garden path.

Spiders crop up often in myth. One of my favourites, is the Cherokee myth of the creation. When the earth was still in darkness, all the animals went to look for the light. They found the sun at the bottom of a hollow tree. Many animals tried to get it out but all failed until the spider came along, and spun a web around the sun to lift it out. Then it could travel to its place in the sky. But the spider was very cunning. In a corner of her web she kept a fragment of the sun so that people could have fire.

My thoughts then turned to the third meaning of the web. As an alternative healer I read many books about different healing traditions, and shamanism is one which draws me back again and again. They use the metaphor of a web to explain how we are all connected to everything else. They see our connections as fine light threads emanating from our body, connecting us to each person or object of importance. It is reflected in our own language with sayings such as 'cutting the apron strings', 'breaking free' etc. It explains why it feels physically painful when we lose someone or something we are especially attached to. Spiders' webs have been a traditional ingredient in many 'witches' brews' and are now being found useful in modern healing techniques. They are now being used in assisting the healing of skin grafts.

With these thoughts in my head, the internet suddenly seemed much more spiritual and less modern. Like all things, of course, its purpose can be diverted and treated as just a mechanistic tool, but I feel that even things like PCs have their own 'energy' about them. Mine has a habit of letting the screen go black for a few seconds if I have been working for a long time without a break. It reminds me that my absorption in what I am writing is also taking away my awareness from my back, which starts aching slightly at the end of a day's typing. It would seem that my back and my PC have telepathic communication with each other. I walk around my garden to straighten my back, before returning to work on a now fully illuminated screen.

The internet web has really cast itself wide, connecting anyone who wants to be connected across the planet. Its potential for breaking down barriers and speeding up information sharing is phenomenal. This new web has so much power to bring about change, which is the work I do for clients. I hope that this new and amazing tool will help us change into a planet of interconnectedness where we all start to care for each other in different ways, where distances of thousands of kilometres become only a few minutes away, showing that we are all part of the worldwide web, the fine strands connecting us to the planet we share.

For clients who come to see me, suffering from depression, it is this sense of everything being connected that they have severed in themselves. They feel lost and unable to make real contact with anyone else, gradually becoming more and more isolated. They feel they are deserted but in fact it is themselves doing the rejecting; they are cutting their own web strands which connect them to everyone else. I first work to put them back in touch with themselves, since we can only have good connections with other people when we have a full and open connection with ourselves and our own inner thoughts and feelings. This is what causes the sense of healing and inner calm which those who commit themselves to working with me find. This is what I found from my own experience and is the basis of shamanistic forms of healing for mental illness and emotional difficulties.

Some people feel threatened by the beginnings of reconnection because they have become strangers to themselves. Sometimes they tell me that I am not doing the therapy properly and they stop coming. Often they look around and wonder why everyone else seems so involved and they are excluded. This all comes from the fear which drove them from themselves in the first place. The power of negative emotions is so strong you wonder how it will ever be broken. But in the end it will be. Positive thoughts have so much more power than negative ones. They may not seem very organised at first – that comes with time and patience, the tending and nurturing that any garden needs.

Whilst I find the internet web a most useful form of connection, there is no substitute for being connected to yourself, your environment and those around you. And on that note I will now go back out into my garden and watch the spiders rebuilding their webs in the afternoon sunshine. Out there I could never feel isolated from anything because everything is all around me, in all its beauty and continuity. I think that one intention for everyone should be to develop a place where they can feel this sense of real connectedness, both with themselves and with everything and everyone around them. A small phrase used as a daily mantra helps me to remember this. 'I am but a small part of it all, but I am part. I am very much connected.'

# Useful Addresses

Sylvia Clare
Workshops and Seminars
For inclusion on mailing list SAE to
Clatterford House
Clatterford Shute
Carisbroke
IOW PO30 1PD
or visit our website: www.claritybooks.co.uk or ring 01983
537338

Corporation of Advanced Hypnotherapy
PO Box 70 Southport
PR8 3JB

Christine King
Metaphysical Society for the Expansion of Consciousness
PO Box 89
London SE3 7JN

Association for the Scientific Study of Anomalous Phenomena
20 Paul Street
Frome
Somerset BA11 lDX

Wilfred Leng
London Relativity Study Group
22 Birch Tree Walk
Croydon
Surrey CR0 7JY

# Further Reading

*Change Your Mind and Keep the Change*, Connie and Steve Andreas, Real People Press

*Reincarnation and The Dark Goddess*, Rae Beth, Robert Hale Ltd

*Life Patterns Soul Lessons and Forgiveness*, Henry Leo Bolduc, Adventures into Time Publ.

*The Psychic Pathway*, Sonia Choquette, Random House

*Stepping Into the Magic*, Gill Edwards, Piatkus

*Creative Visualisation*, Shakti Gawain, New World Library

*Einstein in 90 minutes*, John and Mary Gribbin, Constable and Co

*The Art of Psychic Protection*, Judy Hall, Findhorn Press Series

*You Can Heal Your Life*, Louise Hay, Eden Grove Editions

*The Science of Mind*, Ernest Holmes, G.P. Putnams, New York

*Love is Letting go of Fear*, Jerry Jampolsky, Celestial Arts, California

*Tarot Plain and Simple*, Anthony Louis, Llewellyn Publications

*I Ching*, Chris Marshall, Headline Book Publishing

*Anatomy of the Spirit*, Caroline Myss, Bantam Books

*Why People Don't Heal and How They Can*, Caroline Myss, Bantam Books

*Sixth Sense – How to unlock your intuitive brain*, Laurie Nadel, Prion

*The Serpent and the Circle*, Namua Rahesha, Piatkus

*The Tibetan Book of Living and Dying*, Sogyal Rinpoche, Rider Books

*Sacred Path Cards*, Jamie Sams, Harper Collins

*Living Intuitively*, Bruce Way, Lothian Publishing, Australia

*Many Lives, Many Masters* and *Only Love is Real*, Brian Weiss, Piatkus

# Index